The Good Teacher's Almanac
How to Become the Teacher
You Always Wished You Had

Tom Smock

Illustrations by Jason Grant
Photographs by Stephanie Blumert

Van Arsdale House Publishing
Stanhope, New Jersey

0-9703718-5-3

Published by Van Arsdale House Publishing
126 Main Street
Stanhope, NJ 07874 U.S.A.

Publisher's Cataloging-in-Publication

Smock, Tom.
    The good teacher's almanac : how to become the teacher you always wished you had / Tom Smock ; Jason Grant, illustrator ; Stephanie Blumert, photographer. -- 1st ed.
      p. cm.
    Includes index.
    ISBN: 0-9703718-5-3

    1. Teaching. 2. Curriculum planning. 3. Classroom management. 4. Teacher-student relationships. 5. Teachers. I. Title.

LB1025.3.S66 2000371.02

                        QBI00-500151

LCCN: 00-133729

Table of Contents

Foreword

Recently, during a week-long summer planning workshop, Tom Smock led a session called Planning for the Big Picture. He asked us, "What do you teach?"

"Write it down," he said. I wrote: English. I looked up. People around me were still writing. I wrote: Humanities, Writing, Literature. *We all know what we teach*, I thought. *What is he getting at?* I looked up again. People were sharing what they had written: Math, Social Studies. Someone said, "Students." *Of course*, I thought, *Students*. Somehow, I had lost sight of it, lost focus. How could it have happened so quickly? I haven't been teaching for very long.

Then Tom asked us, "What do you want your students to become?" Silence. This had nothing to do with our subject matter. Or course proficiencies. We were lost, but not for long. "What do you want your students to become?" he asked again. "Write it down." So we did. We want our students to become self-aware, motivated, problem solvers, critical and creative thinkers, thoughtful contributors, responsible members of society. The room was charged. I felt alive, electric. As we stated each wish for our students, Tom wrote it on the board.

His next question was, "What will you do this year to help your students become these things?" Hmmm. More silence. The room wasn't suddenly charged with frantic writing. This was a difficult question. We had to think on this one. We reacted slowly, talking it out. Gradually, inevitably, we turned to conversation about the amount of time we need to accomplish these goals -- and how few of them appear on proficiency checklists. Tom drew a line down the center of the board. To the right of the line, he began to write our concerns. I looked at the board. On the left was a list of things I really want for my students. On the right was a list of things that typically fill my day. These things, Tom explained, make up the little picture. "If you can put a check mark next to it," he told us, "you can be pretty sure it's little picture stuff. It's easy to begin your planning here. If you check everything off, you think you're in good shape; everything's covered."

"The other side of the board," Tom said, pointing to the left, "is the big picture." It's here, I realized, that teaching begins. It starts with our earliest desires to teach. With the big picture in our hearts, we take on careers in teaching. But it starts to fade, maybe as soon as we enter the classroom. After all, there are so many details to consider. I realized how effectively these details were interfering with what I really want to achieve.

It's easy to lose sight of it, but we must keep coming back to the big picture in order to become what we want to be: good teachers.

I left that session with more focus than all of my years of undergraduate and graduate teacher training had provided. That focus is what this book will help you find. It is the beginning of a thoughtful teaching journey. Whether you start this journey as you begin your teaching career or pick up the trail as a veteran teacher makes no difference. It is the big picture that matters. With this book as your guide, you will discover how to keep that picture in focus.

Sara Bauer-Zingg

x

Preface

This book is intended to be a resource for anyone who wishes to become a successful teacher. It is based, in part, upon the notion that a country whose government is "of the people, by the people, and for the people" should have schools that are of the students, by the students, and for the students. I believe all students can learn. It is my hope that within these pages you find enough collective wisdom to make your classroom the kind of place where students are empowered, and dreams begin to come true.

If you do find wisdom among these pages, it is because teachers who had walked the road before I did took the time to point me in the right direction. Much of what I have written here is simply the "working out" in my own life of what they have "worked in." Throughout my years in the classroom, my greatest help has come from the generosity of these veteran teachers who willingly shared their insights, dreams, and joys, as well as their heartbreaks. Like all great teachers before them, they passed the torch of teaching to me before I was even aware I could carry it. This book is my attempt to carry on that tradition.

I am not the best teacher in my school. I may not even be the best teacher in my classroom. During the fifteen years that I have had the honor of teaching in American high schools, I believe I have learned more from my students than they have learned from me. Yet the one thing I am sure I have learned is also the most important. A teacher's influence never ends. As the years pass, I am aware of this more and more. It was my fifth grade teacher who was the first one to suggest I could write a book. That idea never left me. In a very real way, you would not be reading this page now were it not for her. If you gain one insight from this book, let it be that you are an integral part of the future of each of your students. The ideas you place in their minds and the dreams you nurture in their hearts will help to make them who they ultimately become. It is my hope that this book does the same thing for you.

A few years ago, I was given the opportunity to facilitate the training of new teachers in my school district. As the months passed and we worked our way through training, I found they were most interested in the personal insights I could offer as a colleague who had "seen it all."

While their minds were challenged by the curriculum offered by the district, it seemed their hearts were touched by the anecdotes and personal reflections I had to offer. Countless times they encouraged me to "write this stuff down." So I did.

To make sure I was practicing what I preach, I thought it appropriate to include my students in the production of this book. Therefore, the illustrations and photographs you find in *The Good Teacher's Almanac* were developed by my students. I wish to thank Jason Grant for capturing, with pen and ink, the ideas I wished to express visually. Often I gave Jason nothing more than the faintest of ideas with which to work, yet he continually amazed me with his insightful sketches. Working with Jason reminded me once again why a picture is worth a thousand words. Likewise, I wish to thank Stephanie Blumert, whose photographs grace both the pages of this work and its cover. It was a great honor for me to encourage both of these budding artists in their work.

In addition, I would like to thank the wonderful colleagues with whom I have shared my teaching career. It is their stories which bring these pages alive for me. As you read, I hope you are able to gain some sense of appreciation for the professionalism, love and undying devotion they have shown to their students over the years. While I have changed some names in order to protect privacy, their stories are true. In reading them you will realize what it means to be a dedicated teacher.

Finally, I wish to thank the people who took

me beyond my classroom and helped make sure this book became a reality. I offer a special thank you to my editor, Sara Bauer-Zingg, who not only understood my dream but decided to dream it with me. I will remain forever grateful for her interest in my "big project." Thanks are also in order for Jim Deegan and his staff, who made a loose collection of ideas turn into a book. I greatly appreciate their overlooking my ignorance of layout and design. Most of all, I wish to thank my wife Karla, and my children: Hannah, Daniel, and Nathan. Through fifteen years of teaching and more than a year of writing, they have been my greatest source of support. Thank you for holding on to my dreams with me and for never breaking any of them.

Chapter 1

Test Taking Directions
Read This First!

This is a test.

Today you will begin the Test of Quality Teaching Practices in order to determine your aptitude as a public or private school educator. You will have twenty-five years to complete the test. Please turn your test booklet to the page labeled "test taking directions" and read the directions silently as I read them aloud.

For each of the items presented in the test booklet of your career, choose the answer that best corresponds to your current situation. There is no need to darken your answer completely or to use a #2 pencil, for your circumstances will change continually, requiring constant modification of your approach and the tools you use. As a resource, you may use *The Good Teacher's Almanac*.

Just as your student teaching experience began preparing you for a career in education, *The Good Teacher's Almanac* is designed to help keep you moving in the right direction. This book will help fill in the gaps in your understanding. It is a resource and a tool. Use it to your best advantage.

As you read the book, you will notice that each chapter addresses a key aspect of successful teaching. To accomplish this, each chapter begins with a story, an anecdote, or a pertinent piece of research. This is followed by a section of practical suggestions which will help you maximize your effectiveness in the classroom. Throughout the text, you will notice key questions set apart from the rest of the text. These are perhaps the most important components of the book. Answer them honestly. Discuss them with friends. Do your homework! Your efforts here may well shape the future of your teaching career. Specific practical suggestions are sometimes separated from the text. Your only responsibility here is to apply them as you see fit.

As you proceed with your test, remember that *The Good Teacher's Almanac* is not a cook book. Rather, it is a work of philosophy. It is dedicated to the proposition that a recipe approach to teaching will only work when all students suddenly become exactly alike. Instead, it is an honest look at the most difficult yet rewarding profession there is. You will find it short on techniques but long on ideas. You will not become a good teacher by reading this book. You will become a good teacher when you have spent countless hours mastering your craft. *The Good Teacher's Almanac* will show you how.

As you complete each section of your test, be sure to look back over your work. Answers that were once correct may no longer be. Change them accordingly and as you see fit. If you are unsure of the meaning of any of the test items, feel free to discuss them with your colleagues or the author of this book. When you are sure of your answers, you may move on to the next section of the test and continue working.

Your performance on the Test of Quality Teaching Practices will be scored subjectively. Your score will be based on the success shown in the lives of your former students. You will receive interim reports on your progress, with your final score becoming available shortly after the end of your career.

Are there any questions?

You may begin.

Chapter 2
So You Want to Be a Teacher
Why People Teach (and why they don't)

So you want to be a teacher. Then you should look at some facts.

According to independent research projects conducted by the U.S. Department of Labor, the National Education Association, and others, the average teacher will earn a median income of $34,800 in the year 2000. He will work in an urban or suburban school setting, teaching an average of 5 to 6 classes per day. He will teach 140 students per year, sponsor one extracurricular activity and coach one sport. He will teach a 180 day school year with five additional days added for inservice training and teacher workdays. He will complete a 45 hour work week and spend an additional 15 to 20 hours grading papers, attending school activities, and preparing lessons. Earnings will vary greatly from region to region; a starting elementary teacher in Vermont earns an average of $16,000 while an experienced elementary teacher in northern New Jersey earns nearly $47,000 for doing the same job.

Teachers entering the work force at the turn of the century will find themselves spending more hours processing state and federally mandated paperwork than their predecessors. They will be required to work cooperatively with other teachers on a variety of committees and child study teams. They will work in an environment that has a high expectation of positive results but offers little in the way of autonomy. When surveyed, they will categorize themselves as flexible, creative, and positive. They will face a higher than average level of work-related stress.

Among new teachers entering the teaching field, those who will have the least trouble finding and keeping a job include teachers of science (particularly physics) and mathematics, while those who will have the most difficulty include history and English teachers (particularly white males). Labor experts estimate that by the year 2005, there will be an additional 430,000 teaching jobs available in the United States, with a less than equal number of qualified candidates applying for them.

The average teaching career will last five years.

What will you be doing in five years? If you fit the profile of a typical beginning teacher, you will be looking for a new job. If you plan to last longer, what will separate you from the norm? What will give you the staying power to make a career last for ten, twenty or even thirty years? Why do so few people last this long? If you plan to make a long career of teaching and still enjoy it when you finish, you would be wise to first spend some time considering the reasons people give for leaving the teaching profession. These include, but are not limited to:

Frustration and Burnout:

Among reasons given for leaving the teaching field, frustration is near the top of the list. Frustration's eventual end, teacher burnout, is a real and well-documented phenomenon within the educational community. Faced with unmotivated students, decreasing budgets, growing class sizes, aging school facilities, and unsupportive parents, many teachers simply throw in the towel. These teachers began their careers with high expectations and a strong sense of purpose. They entered the profession because of a desire to "make a difference" in the lives of their students. Upon leaving, they feel the difference they have made is small, especially in light of the extraordinary effort required on their part to maintain a standard of excellence in the classroom.

The reasons for this apparent sense of failure are varied, but in simplest terms, the issue may be one of timing. Much like investing, teaching is an endeavor that requires the passage of time before a return is seen. With regard to students, this takes the form of a time delay between the moment of teacher-student interaction and the eventual realization of its effect. Many students are profoundly influenced by their teachers but do not show it or realize it until many years later. The seeds sown in the classroom may take ten years or more to bloom. If a teacher has already left the profession by then, he will never see the fruit of his labor. Even if he stays in teaching, there is no guarantee his former students will return to update him on life's progress. Teachers who focus on the apparent lack of progress they are making with regard to influencing their students often become frustrated to the point of no return. For them, the effort required to maintain a career in teaching becomes Sisyphian in nature. Tired of pushing their personal boulder up the mountain of educational bureaucracy, they eventually head for the door.

As a new teacher wishing to avoid the perils of teacher burnout, you should develop goals for yourself that are student independent. This way you can provide an opportunity for your own success without worrying about the level of performance your students achieve. For example, you may set a goal to develop an interdisciplinary course of study in cooperation with a colleague from another department. In achieving this goal, you have not only produced something useful, you have also developed a relationship with a fellow teacher, set an example for your peers, and expanded your own knowledge base. You have already succeeded before any student enters the picture. Ultimately, you must set student oriented goals as well, but the ability to achieve success in a variety of educational areas is key to any teacher's long-term emotional well-being. For each year you teach, you should have some concrete, specific endeavor to which you can point with pride and say, "I did that."

Lack of Opportunity:

A second reason many teachers leave the classroom is the apparent lack of opportunity it provides. Unlike many professions where workers can earn promotions, change job titles, or transfer to a better location, most teachers find themselves locked in one employment category for the duration of their careers. While it is true that opportunities exist for teachers who become department heads, mentors for new teachers, and staff development leaders, the basic focus of the teacher remains unchanged. Professionally speaking, once a person becomes a teacher, he remains a teacher and the job itself changes little. For this reason, many individuals leave the profession in an effort to find a new challenge.

It is important to note that people leaving the teaching profession because it lacks opportunity for advancement are not necessarily leaving for an unfortunate reason. Unlike their colleagues who leave teaching because of a high level of frustration, many who leave the classroom in search of additional opportunity remain in the field of education. A very high percentage of school administrators are former teachers. For them, the appeal of making a difference in the life of a student still remains. They simply approach it from a different vantage point.

Whether the unchanging nature of a teacher's job will eventually cause you to look elsewhere for fulfillment depends on your personal temperament. For some, teaching becomes a rut; for others, a groove. One way many teachers avoid the feeling of being stagnated professionally is to look for temporary employment opportunities outside the classroom. This goes far beyond the long honored tradition of working for the summer. It entails using professional training and knowledge in a non-school venue. Many teachers have enhanced their careers by working as consultants for textbook manufacturers, curriculum design companies, and a host of other organizations. Some have used their vast subject knowledge to assist libraries, universities, and think tanks. For any teacher feeling the need to expand his professional experience, the opportunities are essentially limitless.

One related yet surprising reason for teachers to exit the classroom is fame. An interesting but little known fact is that teachers who win prestigious awards for their teaching often leave the profession entirely. Winners of state and national Teacher of the Year awards spend at least a year touring the country after winning. During that time, they receive so many opportunities in other fields that many never step foot in the classroom again. Before you assume that the lack of opportunity available to teachers would not bother you, ask yourself what you would do if becoming Teacher of the Year led to an offer for a dream job. Would you go back to the classroom?

Disillusionment:

Perhaps the most unfortunate reason teachers leave the classroom is disillusionment. Despite the various intrinsic rewards associated with teaching, there are times when the negatives simply outweigh the positives. Most often this occurs when teaching ceases, in the mind of its practitioner, to be an honorable endeavor and instead becomes a political animal that rages out of control. Teachers are by nature an altruistic group. They expect everyone else involved with their profession to be also. Unfortunately, this is not always the case. For every instance in which a student's best interest was represented, most teachers can think of several times in which a student's well-being was undermined by the action of a convenience-minded administrator, a profit-minded teacher's union, or a self-serving parent. Over time, these collective instances wear down the resilience of many teachers. Although they entered the profession believing that the educational system was filled with integrity, they leave feeling it is corrupted beyond repair. Most never bother to look back.

With so many reasons to leave teaching, it is a wonder that anyone chooses it for a career in the first place. Yet every year thousands of new teachers enter the classroom in September. What makes them come? While some will leave, many others will stay and enjoy long and satisfying careers in education. What provides for their success? The answers to these questions will form the substance of our discussion for the next several pages. As you will soon see, the reasons people choose careers in teaching are both varied and complex. They also extend far beyond the clichéd June, July, and August.

Born to Teach

Some people are born to teach. You probably grew up with a few in your neighborhood. When the suggestion was made to "play school," it was always their idea. Before anyone could argue, you found yourself "learning" the alphabet or some other useful tidbit under their loving care. When you grew tired of the game and walked away, they simply lined up their stuffed animals and kept going. These teachers never suffer burnout. In part this may be because they are unable to see themselves doing anything else.

In the teaching profession such individuals are rare, but they do exist. More often than not, they come from a family where one or more members were teachers. Having seen the highs and lows associated with being a teacher, they have made the decision that there could be no better place to build a career. Teachers who were born to teach have the unique intuitive ability to know exactly what to do. While the rest of us would struggle for hours to find the perfect way to approach a subject, these teachers can see the perfect solution immediately. Much like gifted athletes who can do easily what others strive to achieve, these teachers are naturals. If you are a teacher like this, consider yourself blessed.

Redirected Early

In recent years, the trend in education has been for teachers to enter the profession through a somewhat circuitous route. Talk to many educators and you will find that they did not begin their college years with teaching careers in mind. Since most high school seniors are anxious to be done with their schooling, it is perhaps no surprise that this should be the case.

Somewhere along the way, however, many people give teaching serious consideration. Although teachers' salaries lag behind those of other professions, there is something about the experience of teaching that remains attractive. Each year there are thousands of college students who change their majors to education. For most, there was some defining moment that demonstrated to them that this was indeed an appropriate path. Whether they were given an informal opportunity to teach and liked it, or just decided their desire was to work with people rather than products, they came to the conclusion that teaching is an endeavor worth undertaking.

Interestingly enough, there seems to be a characteristic profile for individuals who enter the teaching profession this way. Unlike their counterparts who were born to teach, these teachers chose teaching from a wider variety of options. Teaching was not their only interest, just the one they liked best. As a group they love their subject matter but are not enamored of the job opportunities associated with it. They may be lovers of oceanography who get violently sea-sick, or geographers who hate to travel. In addition, they place a higher value on people than they do on things. While they might love engineering, they believe teaching it to someone is more important than producing a product. Finally, these teachers are individuals who maintain a wide variety of interests. If you take the time to listen, you will soon find that, while they love teaching, they would really like to go to cooking school, or be photographers. Until such time as they are able to do this, they remain focused on giving something back to their students in the same way their teachers did for them.

Paradigm Shifts

In another recent trend, a growing number of educators are choosing teaching as a second career. Having completed careers in other fields, they have decided to share their wealth of knowledge in the public or private school setting. For these individuals, teaching provides a viable alternative to retirement or corporate down sizing. Entering the profession later in life, they offer a unique perspective on life within education and without. They are able to draw on their years of experience in the corporate or professional world. This allows them to share countless insights with their students regarding what life is like "on the outside." This is valuable information for students no matter how it is presented.

The struggle for these teachers comes strictly from not being comfortable working with children. Having worked with adults for most of their professional lives, they sometimes find the adjustment required to work effectively with kids more daunting than they expected. Even so, the necessary transition is invariably made and teachers who bring with them ten to twenty years of experience from outside the educational system are often among the most valuable members of any faculty.

Accidentals

Finally, there are those individuals who

enter the teaching profession in the most unexpected and bizarre ways. Consider as an example a technology teacher from Northern New Jersey. Happy with his job as a designer of trade show displays, he was understandably dismayed when his employer went bankrupt. Finding himself frustrated by the seemingly endless line at the unemployment office, he decided to explore the possibilities behind a door marked "placement services." Upon entering, he found eleven state employees eager to search the local area for job opportunities that matched his skills. Much to everyone's surprise, the State of New Jersey happened to be looking for people with his experience to teach technology courses in public high schools. Without a certificate or any teacher training, he entered the classroom under New Jersey's alternate route certification program. And he loved it. Three years later he is among the most effective teachers at his school. Through twists of fate he left his job. And found his calling.

The Big Reasons

No matter what the reason, you now find yourself at the threshold of your teaching career. Whether you were born to teach or find yourself at this crossroads strictly by accident, you share common ground with every educator who is in search of excellence within his profession. While the pathways that lead to this point may vary, good teachers teach for the same reasons.

If you are to be a good teacher, you must first believe that helping people is your highest calling. Your commitment must be to always help and never harm. Much like a physician who lives by the Hippocratic oath, you must swear to do good first and to do good only. In every case you must do what is most beneficial to your students -- even if it leads to a less positive or comfortable situation for yourself. Teaching is a difficult profession because it is continually committed to helping people and because people do not always want to be helped. Even so, to be a teacher is to be a helper, so help you must.

If you are to be a good teacher, you must also realize that the shaping of your students' character is your responsibility. Recently, there has been a trend in education toward abdicating this responsibility. With the crumbling of the moral consensus in our society, there has been a movement toward finger pointing rather than problem solving. Teachers have been quick to blame the breakup of the family for the lack of character they see among their students. Likewise, parents have been quick to say that schools are not doing their jobs. The reality is that we need each other. Like bookends supporting a row of books, parents and teachers support their students from both sides. If one is missing, there is no stability. As a dedicated and effective professional, you are obligated to hold up your end.

As a good teacher, you must also realize that you are constantly molding your students' ambitions and dreams. Whether you realize it or not, much of their outlook on life will be determined in your classroom. You will either serve to empower them or weigh them down. By encouraging their dreams and refining their ambitions, you are doing them the greatest good. At its foundation, teaching is the profession that leads to all other professions. No matter what course a person chooses for his life, he will at some point need the assistance of a teacher. Good teachers never lose sight of this fact and never underestimate the value of their influence.

It is perhaps this reason for teaching that best incorporates the others. To be a teacher is to be constantly influencing an entire generation of children. Through the students they teach and the people these students know, teachers have the opportunity to touch the entire world. By helping, shaping, molding, and influencing, teachers change the future. They do this because, at a fundamental level, they view what they do as a noble endeavor. Good teachers change the world for good.

If this is your mindset as you start your career, you need only to gain the experience necessary to mold yourself into an outstanding educator. If your reasons for teaching are to help, shape, mold, and influence the hearts and minds of your students, you will do fine. Please read on to find some practical ways to achieve excellence in your new profession.

If these are not your reasons, the book ends here.

Chapter 3
Getting Off to a Good Start
How to Find a Mentor Who Can Help

He should have mined coal but instead he moved south-- from Frogtown, Pennsylvania, past the Mason-Dixon line, to the land of make believe and Mickey Mouse -- Florida. There he taught high school.

I met Lou during the first year of my teaching career. Our paths crossed through twists of fate and declining enrollment. Eight months earlier, the space shuttle had exploded over Cape Canaveral, and by September the children who would have been my students had long since moved away as their families searched for work which the space center no longer provided. In the idyllic sounding town of Palm Bay there was no work for me either. So I packed my briefcase and headed north to Eau Gallie (a blue-collar town whose name means dirty water in French and whose high school is often mistaken for a mausoleum). I arrived in Eau Gallie heading north in much the same way that Lou had arrived heading south.

Twenty years before, Lou had awakened to a blustery Pittsburgh morning and informed his wife that "snow stinks and we're moving." Three days later, they reached their final destination when Lou announced, "This looks nice. We'll stay here." Within a day he had a job, and Eau Gallie High School has never been the same.

My career at Eau Gallie began at the start of the fifth week of classes in 1986. Lou met me at the door. I had four weeks of teaching experience to my credit; Lou had twenty-five years. I was young and idealistic; he was older but with a sparkle in his eye. We stood together in the main office like a contradiction in terms. He, the experienced and mature department chairman, and I, the rookie science teacher with an attitude. I wore blue jeans and a Hawaiian shirt. Cotton was my middle name. Lou wore cowboy clothes from Sears and thought polyester was God's gift to men. For an awkward moment Lou looked me up and down with contempt, then tossed me a set of keys.

"These will get you into room 16-105," he said brushing his way past me.

"Is there anything else you can tell me?" I questioned.

"Yeah, I'm Lou. Good luck."

In the following weeks I learned a great deal about Lou's outlook on life and teaching. If Florida had coal mines, Lou would have been the first in line for work. The coal mines appealed to him. In a coal mine a man knows what's expected -- honest work for an honest wage. His labor is measured by the ton. His wage is paid by the hour. Lou taught children like a coal miner.

Lou was stuck in his ways like a leopard is stuck in his spots. To say that he was rigid would be a monumental understatement.   But unlike most people who fit this description, Lou's actions were not learned behavior. They were an integral part of who he was, a seam in his moral fabric. The faculty voted him least likely to change.   Lou proclaimed himself least likely to need to.

My first conflict with Lou came in the sixth

week of school. Determined to be an innovative science teacher, I had sworn off teaching "by the book." Mine would be a classroom filled with rich experiences, lab work, hands-on activity. Content be damned! We were going to have fun. That Wednesday I taught osmosis and diffusion. The lab was innovative. It was unorthodox. It was loud! Lou watched from the doorway of my classroom as tennis balls and balloons flew past hysterical students in safety goggles. The note in my mailbox following class was simple and to the point: "We don't do things like that around here."

Conflicts with Lou upset me at first until I realized that, at one point or another, he was in conflict with everyone. He was at his confrontational best at faculty meetings. Although he never wanted to attend, Lou could liven up a faculty meeting faster than greased peas on Teflon. According to Lou's way of thinking, people only needed to discuss their ideas when they weren't sure if they were any good. A meeting, therefore, was an invitation to critique -- and no one escaped his scrutiny. Administrators were his favorite target, and Lou's popularity among the faculty rose and fell according to how well he had skewered the latest administrative initiative. More than a few administrative ideas withered under Lou's pronouncement that they were "about as smooth as a turd in a punchbowl."

Perhaps Lou's greatest conflicts occurred with his students. It was here that irresistible force met immovable object. A typical encounter would begin with a confused child leaving his seat to approach the judge's bench of Lou's desk.

"Excuse me, sir?"

Without looking up, Lou would grunt acknowledgement.

"I don't understand..."

Suddenly the child would have Lou's full attention, and more often than not it was more than he bargained for.

"Why not?" Lou would counter, his voice steady but not reassuring.

"Well...I can't seem..."

"Can't? Did you say can't?"

"Yes, sir."

At this point it no longer mattered why the child had bothered to try to ask a question in the first place. He was now a victim of Lou's onslaught, a barrage of questions so intense it left only the strongest standing.

"Are you retarded?"

"No, sir."

"Mentally handicapped?"

"No, sir."

"Problems at home I should know about?"

"No, sir!"

"Well then, remember one thing from this conversation and one thing only. You can, so don't ever say you can't. You can and you will! Now sit down and keep trying."

And some of them did.

Through September, however, there were far more students leaving Lou's class than there were entering. He kept the pressure on all month, searching for the "true vein" of dedicated students.

"Just like mining," he would say. "You throw away the rock and keep the coal." By month's end Lou had found what he wanted: those students who were tough enough to face his criticism. The few. . . the proud. . . the coal miners.

It was to these students that Lou revealed himself. He lived for them and he would have died for them even though he would never admit it. They saw a side of him that only a few did. I am glad to have been among the privileged. I was allowed to see past the storm.

It took two years for Lou to accept me. It happened on a spring afternoon at lunch time. Lunch time was like a religious event for our science department, a chance to put aside the cares of our little world and focus on more important issues. It was in this setting that Lou held court. Topics of discussion ranged from politics to war, famine to welfare. Lou always chose the topic, and Lou always had the last word. On this day, however, a former student came to visit and Lou graciously gave her the floor. She had sat in his class; she had sat in mine. We talked about old times. Before long she began talking about the wonderful lab she remembered from my class, with its balloons and tennis balls, goggles and running students.

"Newfangled garbage," Lou muttered through his tuna fish.

"But that lab was great," she protested. She then proceeded to give the best student summary of osmosis and diffusion that either of us had ever heard. With time running out on the lunch period,

Lou offered his final words for the day. "I guess I was wrong."

From that point on, Lou's relationship with the whole department changed. We had never heard him say he was wrong and it made him seem a lot more human. The armor had been pierced.

The last time I saw Lou try to impose his point of view on the other members of the department was during the Gulf War. Televised scenes of people protesting the war punched all of Lou's angry buttons.

"I wish those hippies would get a job," he said to no one in particular.

"How do you know they're unemployed?" we replied in unison.

"If they had jobs, they wouldn't be out protesting and smoking pot!"

"How do you know they were smoking pot?" we asked.

"I could smell it."

"On TV?!"

"Yes on TV! And plus the fact everybody knows that hippies don't want to work."

The next day we donned our best hippie clothes and asked Lou if we could mow his lawn. He never tried to force his ideas on us again.

Twelve hundred miles now separate me from Lou. I think about him often. There is no way to capture in a few hundred words the complexity of the man or what he has meant to me. There is no one to whom he can be compared. He is one of a kind. He could have been a coal miner but he chose not to be. Instead, he chose to mine for students who would give honest work for an honest wage. To them he taught a coal miner's lesson: If you squeeze the coal hard enough, you'll make a diamond.

We all remember teachers. Whether they were the best we ever had or the worst, they stand out in our minds as icons of a day long past. Family members change. We, ourselves, grow older. Yet in our minds, our teachers remain the same. With the slightest mention of remembrance, we find ourselves once again sitting in their classrooms, transported by our memory to a place and time that helped determine who we are.

Perhaps you once had a teacher like Lou. More than likely, you did not. Undoubtedly, this description caused you to form an opinion of him as a teacher. Maybe you liked him, maybe not. Perhaps he was a little too intense for your taste. If you are like most people, you probably did not appreciate his approach until the story's last sentence. The same can be said of his students. While in his class, they often hated him. Years later, when they realized all that he had done for them, they loved him.

Even if you never had a teacher like Lou, at some point you had a teacher whose influence was just as profound. More than you probably realize, she shaped you as a person. Without her, you would not be where you are today, and most certainly you would not have a desire to be a teacher. For all her efforts you probably offered few words of thanks and, if your story is typical, the teacher who influenced you most has no idea that you are about to become her colleague. Such is the nature of teaching. At its core, it is a profession grounded on faith. Whether she voices it or not, every good teacher believes that the seeds of wisdom she sows into the hearts and minds of her students will someday bloom.

As you begin your teaching career, always keep in mind that you may never see any of the fruits of your labor. At first this sounds like rather a sad thing. Yet, in a larger sense, it is wholly appropriate. If your students were immediately able to apply everything you taught them, it would only mean that you were not teaching them enough. Conversely, if they were never able to apply anything you taught them, you would be teaching them more than they could bear. Somewhere in between is the balance you will need to find if you are to become a good teacher. Unfortunately, the trade-off for this balance guarantees that you will never really know exactly how good you are. Some of the seeds you sow will simply have to bloom in another time and place. In the times of self doubt that will inevitably come, think only of the teachers whose influence on your life extended far beyond your time in their classrooms. Think of Lou.

What Lou became, for those who were fortunate enough to sit in his class or to work with him, was a mentor. He was a trusted friend and colleague in the good times and the bad. While he could be profoundly intimidating to new teachers and students alike, he was also their greatest help and source of wisdom. There are many teachers working in schools today who owe their success to Lou.

As a beginning teacher, you can have no greater asset than a good mentor. Mentors are so vital for new teachers' success that nearly every school district in America assigns them to first year teachers. Some states require it by law. No matter what circumstance applies in your case, you will need a mentor. If one has not been given to you, go out and find one. If you can, get two. Their assistance will prove invaluable. When surveyed, experienced teachers say they learn the most about effective teaching from their colleagues. It will be no different for you.

How to find an effective mentor:

There are a variety of ways to find someone who will guide you through your first year of teaching. The simplest way is to ask. If you have not been assigned a mentor by your principal, put a note in a fellow teacher's mailbox. Start with those who teach similar subjects and then extend your invitation to the faculty at large. You will be amazed at how willing some of your colleagues are to take a newcomer under their wing. While this is the simplest approach to finding a mentor, it is also the technique followed least often by new teachers. Many fear it is like announcing to the entire school that you do not know what you are doing. Don't worry, the faculty already knows this! Do not throw away the chance to work with a quality veteran teacher simply because you are afraid to ask for help.

If the humble plea for help does not appeal to you, there are still other ways to find a guide for your first year of teaching. What follows is by no means an exhaustive list:

Ask your principal.
Administrators know who the good teachers are. They know whom they would want teaching their own kids. So ask them. As a courtesy, remember to always ask them in a professional manner. Never ask an administrator to tell you who the best teacher on staff is. If the situation were reversed, you would not want to be put on the spot like that. Instead, ask your principal who she thinks could offer you the most helpful insights as you begin your career. You will get the answer you want without stepping on anyone's toes.

Ask your students.
Students also know who the good teachers are. They know better than the administrators! They will also tell you in a manner that is surprisingly forthright. Students are highly adept at expressing their opinions, especially regarding teachers. Here you also have the added luxury of being able to ask the question straight out. It is legitimate to ask students who they think is the best teacher in the school. You should also ask them why they hold their opinions. Without realizing it, they may hold a teacher in high regard for all the wrong reasons. Often, however, their insights are right on target and will give you the direction you need. A word of caution: Never ask students who they think is the worst teacher in the school. They will tell you that also!

Listen to your colleagues.
It will not take long for you to hear who is respected by his peers. Teachers with successful techniques are often the topic of lunch room conversation. Keep your ears open.

Look to past history.
Who was last year's Teacher of the Year? What about previous years? How were they chosen? Can there be any better way to ask a colleague for help than to tell him you are seeking his counsel because he has been recognized as among the best?

Search for a kindred spirit.
There is much truth to the old adage that birds of a feather flock together. You will know immediately which colleagues you find appealing and which ones you do not. Trust your judgment.

One final thought about mentors. If you have been given a mentor ahead of time, find out how he was assigned. Was he forced into this by the administration or did he volunteer? Is he excited about being your mentor or would he rather not? These are important questions you must have answered. Be exceedingly courteous but also firm. One sure-fire way to approach this is to ask your mentor what he can show you about how to be an effective teacher. If he hesitates, or if he seemingly does not have very many ideas, you will need more help than your mentor has to offer. You will need to enlist the help of additional colleagues using the strategies previously mentioned.

Chapter 4
Your Teaching Identity
Finding Who You Are as an Educator

The most thought provoking question I was asked during my first year of teaching came from a man who had been teaching for more than twenty years. After being introduced, he graciously welcomed me to my new school and then asked, without irony, "When do you plan to retire?" When I told him I was unsure, he gave me an assignment that proved to be well worth the time.

"Take a week," he said, "and talk to the teachers around here. Find out how long they have been teaching, when they started, and how old they are. Then ask them how they feel about being teachers. When you're done, you'll have an answer to my question."

So I talked to other teachers. As promised,

within a week I knew exactly when I planned to retire. I will be fifty-two. At that point I will have been teaching for three decades. I will have given instruction to over three thousand students, and I will be ready to move on to something else. I do not know yet what that something else will be. Maybe I will write books.

Whether you like it or not, you will not be a good teacher for at least three years. You could be an adequate teacher. You may even be a promising teacher. But you will not be good. Teaching is far too difficult for that.

Your success as a teacher after your first three years will be determined by three things: your natural talent, your willingness to build a good foundation for your career, and your ability to overcome the obstacles that stand in the way of good teaching. Of the three, your ability to overcome is the most important. This having been said, it is still worthwhile to look at all three in some detail.

Your Natural Teaching Ability

Some people are born teachers. Through no effort of their own, they are blessed with all the character qualities that make for good teaching. They are quick thinkers. They are comfortable before large groups of people. They are able to adapt to any circumstance. From the very start of their careers, they will seem to lead a charmed life.

For most of us, however, teaching does not come so easily. It requires hours of hard work. Ironically, your own innate ability is the one aspect of your teaching over which you have the least control. True, you can improve your ability to teach through practice, but there is little you can do to make yourself a "natural." Therefore, it is a worthwhile exercise to honestly assess your strengths and weaknesses before you get too far into your teaching career. Since you have yet to gain a wealth of experience in teaching, what you may find yourself assessing is your own personality rather than your teaching prowess. This is still a good thing to do. What type of person are you? Do you take things in stride or are you nervous when things vary from the plan? Are you organized to a fault, or do you have a flair for improvisation? In your dealings with students, what do you wish to establish first: respect or rapport? By asking yourself questions like these, you will gain insight into what type of teacher you will probably become. In addition, you will form a mental picture of how you want your classroom to operate. Such a self assessment will help you in two ways. By honestly assessing your strengths and weaknesses, you will be able to better understand your successes and failures within the classroom. On a day when everything seems to go right, you may find that you were working in a way that favored all your strong points. Similarly, a bad day may find you dabbling in areas where you are weak. If you have looked at yourself honestly, you will have given yourself a useful diagnostic tool which will allow you to maintain your ability in areas where your performance is strong, while also allowing you to strengthen the areas in which your performance is lacking.

Second, an accurate self assessment of your strengths and weaknesses allows you to begin developing a vision for the ideal cultural climate you wish to establish in your classroom. Obviously, you want to play to your strengths while minimizing your shortcomings. With this in mind, you could consciously work toward developing such an atmosphere in your classroom. Your class will become what you make it, and you will shape it according to your own desires and personality. While you may never be able to change the level of your natural ability, there are still a thousand ways to get the most from it. Even a "natural" has many hours of work to do. As you work to become the excellent teacher that you wish to be, consider what jazz great Louis Armstrong once said when asked how he could play his trumpet so effort-lessly. Said Armstrong, "I work very hard to make it look very easy."

Building a Good Foundation

Working very hard to make it look very easy begins with building a strong foundation for your career. Building a good foundation for your career begins with a decision regarding the type of teacher you wish to be. This goes beyond simply being a "good teacher" and strikes at the core of your personality. Below are profiles of actual teachers and their approach to their profession. Read them carefully before answering the questions which follow.

DOUG

Doug teaches physics. More specifically, he teaches the love of physics. All that he is as a teacher flows forth from his love for his subject matter. Upon starting his career, he took over a stagnant physics program in a medium-sized high school and within one year tripled its enrollment. To further spark student interest, he formed a physics club and hosted "star parties" in order to give students their first chance to look at the heavens through a telescope. Enrollment contin-ued to grow. A second physics teacher was needed, then a third. Yet Doug's greatest encouragement comes when some of his students choose physics as their college major.

SUSAN

Susan teaches students. She also teaches psychology. Susan enters her school each morning with only one objective: to serve kids. To this end she has, over the course of her career, established a drug counseling service, invited students to her home, been a class advisor, coached cheerleading, mentored independent study projects, and served on countless committees which had as their focus student services. If, at the end of the school year, she has covered her course material, she considers it a bonus. Yet, if any student leaves her class unsure of her love for them, she considers herself a failure. Her colleagues have shown their confidence in her by electing her Teacher of the Year for three years in a row.

WAYNE

Wayne teaches order. He begins before he has even said one word. Desks in Wayne's room are placed in rows according to color. Wall decorations are content-related, crisp, clean, and evenly spaced. Pencils in his desk drawer are arranged by length, tallest to shortest, each with a perfectly sharpened point. Every day, class follows the same procedure: a brief review, an introduction of new material, questions regarding homework, sample problems from the textbook. Timing is to the minute. Each night involves the same number of homework problems to be completed according to the prescribed method. Students who closely follow Wayne's method say that he has made math understandable to them in a way no one else ever has. When informed of this Wayne smiles and says, "Of course."

PAT

Pat teaches respect. More importantly, he commands it. As much as any member of the faculty, Pat is considered "old school." In his case, "old school" is a compliment. Pat is known by every student within the school as the most demanding member of the faculty. His tests are notorious, his in-class demeanor more so. Students can not pass his class without earning extra credit. Their assignment? To attend the school play. Or the conference championship for girls' basketball. Or any other event where Pat has determined that students are giving their all in an activity that might go unrecognized. So his students attend fencing matches and chess tournaments. In droves. And they bring their friends. They learn that people who give their best effort are worthy of respect. And Pat smiles a confident smile and considers himself a success.

What about you?

What kind of teacher will you be? What kind of teacher do you wish to be? Your answers to these questions will be unique. You, after all, are an individual. You are unlike anyone else on the face of the earth and you will teach accordingly. Your answers will shape your entire career.

Yet most beginning teachers would be hard-pressed to answer either question. Envisioning _y will become as teachers is beyond their ability. With the pressures of lesson planning, paper grading, and classroom management constantly on their minds, keeping their heads above water seems a more pressing concern than considering what they will be like as veteran teachers.

Yet teaching, more than most professions, requires such a long-term view. With the daily pressures associated with the job always vying for your attention, it is too easy to allow your teaching identity to be developed by default. This is a sure-fire recipe for dissatisfaction. As a beginning teacher, you cannot afford to neglect the development of your professional identity. If you do, you will be like the unfortunate player who throws his darts before the board is hung, desperately hoping that the bullseye will appear in the right place! You must not make this mistake. You will never know if you have arrived unless you first establish your destination. To help you get started, consider the following questions:

Theory Into Practice

To help establish your own teaching identity, begin by examining the personalities of other teachers.

Which of the teachers profiled did you identify with most strongly? Why?

If you had to be just like one of these teachers, which one would you choose?

How are these teachers similar?
What makes them unique?

ning **What Stands in Your Way**

Having maximized your natural ability and worked hard to establish a good foundation, you need to do one more thing in order to be successful in your teaching career. You must overcome what stands in your way.

In an ideal world, nothing would stand in the way of a conscientious teacher trying to do her job. Unfortunately, the world you are about to enter will offer a much different reality. Since this is the case, you should do everything in your power to make the following statement a part of your professional mindset: "Teaching selects towards those individuals who minimize an energy loss." Commit this to memory. Understand what it means. Apply it at every opportunity.

Notice first that it does not say that teaching selects towards those individuals who minimize energy use. Teaching is an energy intensive job. It requires a great commitment on the part of its practitioners. No matter how you approach it, teaching will be draining at times. Good teachers are not lazy. They cannot afford to be.

Yet teaching is unique among professions because it offers intrinsic rewards unavailable in any other line of work. Being a good teacher is fun. It is rewarding. It is rejuvenating. When it goes well, there is no better job in the world.

This is the real dynamic of teaching. For every circumstance that can tear you down, there is another that can build you up. The reverse is also true. With the exception perhaps of professional athletes, teachers can move from the highest highs to the lowest lows faster than any other type of employee. The trick, if you wish to remain for the long run, is to keep the energy ledger balanced.

How can you do this? How can a teacher make sure she maintains a surplus of positive energy? Consider the following principles:

Don't worry about trivial matters:
One of the most common mistakes beginning teachers make is to strive for perfection in areas where perfection is unnecessary. You will be tested on this the first time you find a typographical error on a handout of which you just made 200 copies. If you find yourself wondering whether you should correct the mistake and run off new copies, you are taking yourself entirely too seriously. Do everything in your power to avoid mistakes, but when you make them move forward, not back. Make a joke about the typo with your students and have a good laugh. You may even find they like you better as a result. (Just make sure you fix the handout before next year.)

Maintain forward momentum:
Since new teachers tend to be focused on doing things exceedingly well, they are prime candidates for getting sidetracked when things go poorly. Many times it is difficult for a new teacher to bounce back following a lesson that has gone poorly, or from a confrontation with a student or a

parent. If you find yourself in this situation, be sure to keep the long-term picture in constant focus. Ultimately, you will spend nearly 200 days with your students during the year. They will have bad days and you will forgive them. Make sure you remember to expect the same favor in return. In the long run, your students will remember you for your consistent approach to teaching. You will find it surprising how little they will remember of the times when you thought you were at your best. Fortunately, they will tend to forget your low points as well. When all is said and done, they will form an opinion of you that is based on the long term view. They will remember that your class was "good." They will remember the big picture. You should too. If you stumble along the way, just make sure you get up and keep going.

Beware of labor saving devices:
Whether you realize it or not, much of what you will do during the school day will have little to do with actual teaching. Attendance, grade keeping, administrative conferences and dozens of other responsibilities all serve to fill your day with tasks that offer little benefit to your students. When it comes to handling such items, simple is best. Develop a simple system for handling the mundane chores of the workday world and stick with it. Allow a student to take attendance. Use a simple grading system. Remember that all labor saving devices are not effective. Never use a computer unless it offers you an advantage. Often

it takes more time to format something on a computer than it does to write it out by hand. If this is the case in your situation, it is only worth using the computer if the item can be saved and used for years to come. If an item that could be written in five minutes takes an hour to produce on the computer, you will not break even for twelve years! Rather than minimizing your energy loss, you will be leaking like a sieve.

Remember that isolation kills:
Years ago, Simon and Garfunkel reminded us through song that a rock feels no pain and an island never cries. Rocks and islands make lousy teachers! No matter what circumstance you face during your years of teaching, nothing will take the life out of you faster than isolation. Teaching, by its very nature, requires interaction. If you find yourself isolated from your students in any way, you will soon find yourself unable to reach them effectively.   Any chance of receiving positive feedback from your students will be gone and you will find your energy flowing out while there is little or none returning. Without relationships, there is no teaching. Know your students. If they know how much you care, they will care how much you know.

Theory Into Practice

In the long run, you will want to establish a number of positive qualities in your classes. As a beginning teacher, however, you need to pick a starting point. For each of the following, choose the quality you would rather have present in your classroom, and work to establish it.

As you begin your career,
would you rather have. . .

respect or rapport?
order or freedom?
laughter or quiet?
control or risk?
intellect or emotion?
consistency or variety?

Three Steps Toward Teaching Excellence

Now everything is in place for you to become an excellent teacher. You have looked honestly at your own ability. You know your strengths and weaknesses. You have established a good foundation for your career by identifying the type of teacher you long to be and putting things in place to help yourself reach your goal. You know that you must minimize your energy loss and have taken steps to do just that. And for three years you still will not be a very good teacher. Why? Because you have yet to learn the first lesson of successful teaching. You must learn to say "NO."

During your first year of teaching, you will interact with students, parents, and administrators. With students your overriding concern will be gaining their acceptance. To this end, you will do countless things to convince them that you are on their side. They will take advantage of you accordingly. Looking back over your first year, you will think of dozens of circumstances where you should have been more firm, more strict, more diligent. You will file this away in your mind as just another of life's learning experiences and begin to get ready for the next year.

With regard to parents, your overriding concern will be gaining their respect. You know full well that when Johnny or Susie heads home with an unacceptable report card that it will be "all your fault" because "you're new and don't know what you're doing." Therefore, in meetings with parents you will make sure that you are the consummate professional. At every turn you will have a ready justification for your actions. Yet you will still lose. Parents will recognize your vulnerability and they will press until you capitulate. In the worst cases, your administration will need to bail you out. You will then head home replaying the entire encounter over in your mind until you are sure of all the things you should have said. You will be ready for them next time.

When it comes to administrators, your overriding concern will be keeping your job. You will be fearful of saying no to anything they suggest. As a result, you may find yourself coaching three sports, running the spring musical, and driving the late bus. At year's end you will realize that you simply cannot do everything you have been asked and you will reluctantly resign from some of the extracurricular positions to which you had been assigned. Much to your chagrin, you will be called to the principal's office just like you were when you were a student. There you will find your principal much more understanding than you expected. On your way home, you will realize the reason for this. The next school year will bring a fresh crop of new teachers.

During the summer between your first and second years, you will realize how much simpler your rookie year would have been had you said "no" more often. "No" to the students who wanted to take advantage of you. "No" to the parents who challenged your competency. "No" to the administrators who filled your plate to overflowing. Life would have been so much easier if you had just said "NO!"

Yet recognizing your need to be more assertive is not the same thing as knowing how to do it effectively. To learn how, you will need to teach for a second year. In the summer between your second and third years, you will realize you have all the tools you need. During your third year, you will begin to use them. Thus the training period of

your career will be complete. The development
goes as follows:

First Year:
Learned I need to say "no."

Second Year:
Learned how to say "no."

Third Year:
Said "no."

Congratulations! Everything is now in place for
you to become an excellent teacher!

Theory Into Practice

As a final activity for this chapter,
consider the following:

What would your teacher profile say?

Write your own teacher profile, or one for an
influential teacher you have had.

Chapter 5

The Big Picture
How to Think Like a Teacher

Today is Affirmation Monday, a long-standing tradition in my class.

Affirmation Monday began many years ago when one of my students did something tremendously nice just for the sake of making everyone's lives a little bit better. Duly impressed, I made it a point to recognize his effort in class the following day by saying thank you. I fully expected that to be the end of it.

I did notice, however, that he seemed hesitant when I offered my words of appreciation, almost as if he were unsure of what to do. Finally he offered a weak "you're welcome" in response. Meanwhile, the other members of the class sat in puzzled silence, as if they had just witnessed the arrival of a three-armed man. As I often do with things that happen during the school day,

I pondered his reaction late into the night.

The following day, Eric's class arrived at the appointed time in the usual way. Slowly they found their way to their seats, dropped their bookbags beneath their desks and opened their notebooks. I jumped right into the day's lesson. Ten minutes in, I realized my students were a bit sluggish. I became more animated in an effort to liven them up. They became more distracted. Quickly, I moved about the room, involving students in the lesson by "volunteering" them as helpers with demonstrations. They groaned, but their energy level began to rise. Mine, however, was waning. At the halfway point of the class I feared that I had lost them for the day. Even though they had begun to give honest effort, they seemed like their minds were a thousand miles away. Turning my back to the class, I began to sketch something on the chalkboard. Suddenly I heard Eric's voice.

"Can I ask you a question that's off the topic?" he asked.

At this point I was willing to try anything. Turning back to face the class, I looked into Eric's eyes and nodded my head affirmatively.

"Why did you thank me yesterday?"

"What?"

"Yesterday! During class. You thanked me for my help the other day. How come?"

Puzzled, I wondered why Eric was asking this now. Frowning with confusion, I hesitated, then blurted out the only answer that came to mind.

"Because I wanted to."

"But why did you want to?" came the voice, not from Eric this time but from Norm who sat across the room.

Turning my head toward Norm, I saw him sitting forward in his seat, his eyes looking intently toward me, waiting for an answer. Looking back, I saw Eric watching and waiting for my response as well. So were the other students. Life had come back to the class.

"What are you guys talking about?" I asked.

Exasperated, Norm began to spell it out for me, slowly and emphatically, as if he wanted to make sure I understood.

"Yesterday," he began, "you took time out of class to thank Eric for helping you. Teachers never do that. Why did you?"

Stunned by his statement, I stammered out an explanation.

I explained how Eric's actions had been exceedingly generous and how they had made things better for me as well as all of his classmates. I continued by telling how impressed I was that Eric was willing to give up his own time in order to do something for which he would gain no direct benefit. Then I expressed appreciation for the maturity Eric had shown as he and I talked while working together. Satisfied that I had made my point, I looked at Norm and offered a raised eyebrow and a shrug of my shoulders. I was unsure what else to say. For a moment, a thoughtful silence fell over the room.

"Why don't all teachers do that?" asked Stephanie.

Surprised by a question coming from another student, I looked toward her and thought quickly about how to answer. Try as I might, I could not think of an appropriate response. Feeling bewildered, I offered my final statement of the day.

"I don't know."

"They should," she replied.

With that the bell rang, ending class. In silence, looking more mature than their years would allow, my students filed silently out of my classroom and on to their waiting weekend.

By the following Monday, I had given many hours thought to the events of the previous Friday. Most significantly, I had realized that my students had been deeply touched by the events of the preceding week. What I had thought was a simple and appropriate expression of thanksgiving had become a source of great introspection for all of us. As they entered my room, I could see by their faces that we were not yet done discussing this topic.

To be honest, we discussed it for that entire Monday morning class. We continued for part of Tuesday. As a class, we did not move on until everyone had their chance to express their thoughts, feelings and concerns in whatever way they felt comfortable. When silence once again came to the class, I asked if anyone had left anything unsaid. Contemplatively, the class looked around the room at one another. Finally, after a few moments of silence, Eric raised his hand to speak. I acknowledged him with a nod.

"Just one thing," he began, "I would like everyone here to feel what I felt when you said thank you."

And so Affirmation Monday began, and then became a tradition. Each Monday for the remainder of the year, I took ten minutes of class time and devoted it to telling one of my students the things about them that I most appreciated. The other members of the class sat attentively, in respectful silence, until I was done. Then they clapped.

With one Monday to spare, I had managed to offer words of encouragement and affirmation to every student in my class that year. I felt this was entirely appropriate, for the one final Monday the year held offered me an opportunity to affirm them as a group and to thank them for being the best class I had ever taught. Naturally, my students had other plans. When the final Monday of the year came, my students entered my classroom two days away from being high school graduates. Without hesitation, they let me know that this day they would be running the show. One by one, they proceded to stand before the class and affirm one another, adding their own commentary to what I had spoken in earlier months. Finally, with time running out on the class and the year, a student named Dave stepped from his seat and handed me a small gift-wrapped box on behalf of the class.

"We thought a gift would affirm you," he said.

Smiling, he returned to his seat.

"Wow, a new car!" I quipped.

"Well, the keys anyway," came Stephanie's quick reply.

For a brief moment my heart skipped a beat as I realized that she might not be kidding. I looked in her eyes but she gave nothing away. I looked quickly to the other students. No one flinched. To this day, twelve years later, they remain one of my favorite classes of all time. I think of them every Monday.

Today, my classes still love Affirmation Monday. Although they say that it is corny and that it sounds like a promotion for a long distance phone company, they refuse to let me forget it. As the time approaches each Monday I can see the anxious glances of my students toward the clock on the wall as they wait and wonder who will be honored on that particular day. Ironically, it has had an effect on my classes that I would have never thought possible. Monday is now the best day of the week!

Why do I share this? Why admit to devoting class time to something many people would deem impractical? Because I am much like Eric. I want every teacher to feel what I feel when I say thank you to my students.

By the way, they bought me a watch.

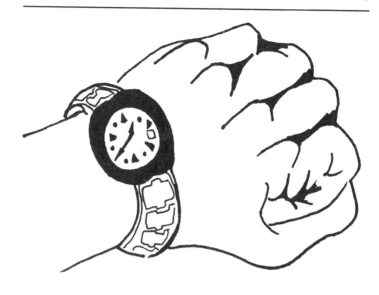

Excellent teaching is transcendent. For the teacher who practices it, the whole is most assuredly greater than the sum of its parts. To "arrive" as an excellent teacher, you must remember that there is a "big picture" that makes teaching both a profession and an art form. To become excellent at your profession, you must first make sure you are viewing it correctly. This begins by asking the right questions. Where should you begin the educational process? How can you, as a conscientious teacher, plan for success?

As a starting point, you must remember that your success as an educator lies beyond the curriculum. The biggest mistake you can make is to think too small. This is a subtle error but a significant one. Typically it will take shape at the point when you sit down, planbook in hand, and n to sketch out your year. While it is tempting to look first at what you want your students to learn, this is often the worst possible place to begin. By starting here, you guarantee only that your students will gain no more from you than from a textbook or encyclopedia. You reduce the entire classroom dynamic into a simple exchange of facts. While quality curriculum is necessary for success in teaching, it is only a means to an end, not the end itself. It is the teacher, not course content, that drives the engaging classroom.

For any teacher, planning plays a vital role in his ultimate success. A teacher who can plan, execute, and refine quality lessons is a credit to his profession. Yet it is a mistake to assume that quality lesson plans will automatically lead to quality teaching. Were this the case, anyone could be a master teacher if he could simply purchase an adequate recipe to follow. You know this is not the case.

Rather than formulating your plan of action by looking to what your students will learn, focus instead on what they will be. Ultimately, your goal as an educator is to develop and facilitate human beings, not disseminate information. Since this is the case, your planning should begin and end with your students, not with your subject matter. Throughout the school year, your goal should remain the development of your students. The subject you teach simply provides the vehicle by which you arrive at your destination. If your goal, at the start of the school year, is to cover the course content, you have missed the big picture.

Rather than focusing on the progress of your students, you will have turned your attention to the conveyance of the curriculum. This denies the vital role your students play in the evolution of their own learning. Remember that without students, teachers become superfluous. When asked what you do, say teach. When asked what you teach, say students.

So what do you want your students to be? In answer to this question, nineteenth century educator Charlotte Mason stated, "people with something to do, something to think about, and something to love." Research in the twentieth century validates her educational philosophy. In numerous studies, students with "something to do" prove more successful than their counterparts who learned passively. In addition, those who are continually challenged with thought provoking material show a tendency to increase their academic performance in similar measure to the challenge provided. Likewise, those given "something to love" (from plants to pets) show greater levels of empathy, compassion, and caring. With this simple philosophy Mason was able to define her ultimate hope for her students without a single mention of subject matter. There is virtually no limit to the goals you can establish for your students. Remember, however, that these goals must focus on changes which occur within the students themselves.

To start yourself thinking along these lines, consider how you might teach a group of students entering a high school physics class. Somewhere within your curriculum there would undoubtedly be some reference to Newton's Laws of Motion. If you focus strictly on subject matter, the progression of your students' learning and involvement begins with the "facts" regarding Newton's Laws. Most likely, you would present these facts through one or more conventional approaches to teaching including lectures, problem solving, and lab work. If this is done effectively, your students will be well versed in the concepts associated with Newtonian physics. Undoubtedly, they will be able to solve a wide variety of problems from the textbook. They will also be able to pass tests related to the subject at hand. Perhaps they will even be able to make appropriate inferences from data collected in the laboratory. From a content oriented perspective you will be able to consider yourself a success.

But what is the true value of this type of success? Research has consistently shown that students who maintain a "just the facts" approach to learning often lose their "learned facts" shortly after they are tested. Also, they show little ability to relate course material to authentic situations they face in life. Thus, their school knowledge becomes separate and distinct from real world knowledge, leaving teachers with a troubling question: If content has little or nothing to do with a student's life outside of school, of what value is it?

Rather than answer this question, consider what would happen if you taught Newton's Laws of Motion to the same group of students while also giving them something to do, something to think about, and something to love. With regard to the "doing" of Newton's Laws, students could be provided a wide variety of lab experiences related to the subject matter. As an introduction, they could complete several lab activities that follow the conventional "cookbook" approach offered by so many textbook publishers. These activities (which are designed to provide textbook results) would provide the foundation for the students' understanding.

From here, you could introduce students to lab work where the results are less predictable. This serves a dual purpose. Not only does it cause students to realize that nature is not always as neat and predictable as the textbook implies, it also forces them to connect their learning to a tangible reality. It also forces students to think critically and to solve problems for which there are no textbook answers. This will develop skills that will serve them well in the years following their school career.

This connection between the tangible reality of the physical world and the completion of student lab work leads directly to the "thinking" portion of your students' learning. Here, students are prompted to examine connections between what they have learned and what they continually see throughout their lives. At this point it is a good practice to refer students to some common experience which they all share and show them how the subject matter in question applies. In the case of

Newton's Laws, there are countless examples for the students to consider.

If you really want to make your students think, you must use scenarios that go beyond those they might expect. The only key is to make sure the examples chosen provide an opportunity for students to connect their classroom learning to the world with which they are familiar. Cartoons might be a good place to start. Students are well aware that cartoon characters often defy the laws of physics, but they rarely realize how often these characters obey them. Having students analyze cartoons by looking for accurate portrayals of physical law allows them to apply their new learning to something with which they are entirely familiar. This allows for connections to develop which enable students to make their learning permanent. By providing students this opportunity, you allow them to "think" the course-related material into their everyday lives. Once there, it will never be lost.

All that remains to be done is for you to provide your students the opportunity to learn to "love" the material in some way. For this to happen, material must be made memorable in a positive fashion. The best way for you to accomplish this is to move the learning environment beyond the walls of your classroom. Once your students realize that every setting provides an opportunity to learn physics, they will begin to develop a positive feeling toward the subject. If they see physics applied in their everyday lives, they will find it enjoyable, relevant, and intellectually challenging. If their learning is limited to the classroom, however, they will not view the learning of physics as a worthwhile pursuit.

In an attempt to make physics something for their students to love, many physics teachers across the United States have in recent years begun taking their students to amusement parks in order to observe physics in action. This is a tremendous example of Mason's educational philosophy at work. By providing thought provoking experiments to conduct while riding on roller coasters and Ferris wheels, these teachers give their students much to do, and many concepts about which to think. In addition, they allow their students to have a great deal of fun. They provide students an opportunity to associate profound enjoyment with the subject matter they are attempting to teach. What better approach to teaching could there be?

Theory Into Practice

Research indicates that people are best able to remember a goal or objective if it is expressed in a phrase no longer than twenty-five words. To help develop your "big picture" outlook, complete the following exercise: Write a statement of no more than twenty-five words which describes what you desire your students to become. In writing this "vision statement," you will create your own personalized version of Charlotte Mason's "Do-Think-Love" theme. You will also have provided a sure-fire way of evaluating whether or not your teaching is transcending the curriculum. If you are able to see your students display the character development you desire for them, you can be sure that you have been a success as a teacher.

A Final Thought Regarding the Big Picture

The ultimate goal of any teacher is to be successful in his teaching. Yet defining success in teaching is an inherently difficult thing to do. Measuring this success is even tougher. Success simply means too many different things for too many different people.

There is common ground, however, upon which we can all agree. Ultimately, people only consider themselves successful if they believe they have reached their goals. No matter what their level of accomplishment, they are not successful unless they have some degree of satisfaction with their level of achievement. As a teacher, you must find a way to get yourself to this point. As a good teacher, you must find a way to get your students there also.

To help yourself and your students maintain a healthy view of learning's big picture, make a habit of setting goals. Research indicates that people who consider themselves "successful" demonstrate a propensity for goal setting not found among those who feel unsuccessful. In addition to articulating goals, successful people are adept at evaluating the attainability of these goals, and developing plans to achieve them. If you encourage this habit among your students, and practice it yourself, you will be teaching your students the very secret of their future success. Finally, give your students something to do, something to think about and something to love. Not only is this the secret to effective teaching and learning, it is a recipe for a happy and fulfilled life. By providing this direction for your students, you will help them gain a healthy and confident perspective on their lives and their futures. There could be no better way for you to affirm them.

Theory Into Practice

Write five goals you have as a teacher. Explain how you will know if you attained each one. After you have established them in their final form, print them neatly on a large sheet of paper. Once you have done this, place them in a location you will not forget. Review your goals each payday. Be sure that you make consistent progress.

Chapter 6
The Classroom Community
Building Rapport with Your Students

On the happy day that I learned my teaching experience would include raising children of my own, I was given some of the best teaching advice I have ever received.

"Never tell your kids no," came the counsel from one of my former college professors.

"What are you talking about?" I responded. "They'll be spoiled rotten!"

"I didn't say not to correct them," he replied. "Just never use the word 'no.'"

As he continued his explanation, I quickly saw the wisdom of his approach. Rather than correct my children with a harshly spoken "no," I would be much wiser to articulate my wishes in a more specific fashion. If I did not want my children to touch something, that is exactly what I should tell them. "Don't touch" is far more clear in providing direction to a toddler than a simple "No!" In addition, parents who raise their children in this way have the added blessing of having their child's first word be something other than the dreaded negative.

It did not take long for me to realize that the same principle could (and should) be applied in the classroom. Students, who enter a class with no knowledge of my desires or expectations, need clear direction regarding what is expected of them. Nothing should be left to chance. Rather than assume a student knows what I am saying, it is far better to be sure. "Hey, don't do that!" may get a student's attention, but "Don't squeeze the gerbils!" lets him know why I wanted it in the first place.

Over the past fifteen years, it has been my practice to employ this sage advice in my classroom. Whenever I need to provide direction to my students, I make it a point to explain my position thoroughly and to articulate my expectations as well. I can tell you it works. How does it work? It works by providing clear and appropriate direction to a person who needs exactly that.

Why does it work?

Because I said so.

* * *

You will not sleep on the night before school starts. As you lie awake listening to the ongoing chatter in your mind, one question will dominate your thinking: How will I keep these kids under control?

If there is one fear that is pervasive among new teachers, it is the fear that they will not be able to handle the rigors of managing a class full of students. While their conscious mind continually reminds them that their students are human beings, their subconscious harbors fears that somehow these kids might really be ravenous little monsters ready to eat them alive. The truth lies somewhere between these two extremes.

With this in mind, it is worthwhile to devote a chapter of this book to developing good relationships with the students you will be teaching. Of the variables which will determine your success as an educator, none will have as profound an impact as effective classroom management. This chapter will show you how to manage your classroom well.

To do this, it will first examine the validity of three clichés of the teaching profession associated with teachers and how they relate to students. This will be followed by five foundational principles which will allow you to build a good rapport with your students. Finally, the chapter will conclude with twelve practical suggestions for implementing these principles in your classroom.

Three Clichés of the Teaching Profession
Cliché #1:
Students don't care how much you know
until they know how much you care.

Of all the clichés spoken of education, this is perhaps the one that rings most true. It is also what makes teaching such a difficult and challenging profession. Regardless of the level of expertise teachers bring to the classroom, they will be found lacking if they are unable to persuade their students that they care. If students do not believe that their best interests are being served in a classroom, their teacher is in for a fight.

This should really not be too much of a surprise. Each of us enters a given situation with a view toward how it will benefit us in the long run. This is doubly true of students because they are often a captive audience within the classroom setting. For the most part, students are in school because they must be, not necessarily because they choose to be. Because of this, students are quick to ask, "What's in this for me?"

Ideally, what is in it for them is quality instruction provided by a caring, empathetic teacher. Not only will the teacher be able to increase their level of understanding regarding the subject at hand, but he will also be able to be an advocate for them as they progress through their adolescent years. Of these two priorities, the second is the most important. While it is true that a teacher is evaluated on the basis of his ability to effectively deliver course content, the part he plays as a supporter and defender of his students plays a far more significant role in influencing his students' lives. In addition, the establishment of a good student-teacher relationship is a prerequisite for any true learning that will take place.

It is a mistake, however, to think this means that students and teacher must become friends before learning can take place. In fact, it is a mistake that many new teachers make. New teachers often waste valuable time and effort in an attempt to win over their students as friends. Students have no such need. They do not need you to be their friend; they only need you to be someone on whom they can rely. If they adopt you as a friend, it is an added blessing. Yet the truth of the matter is that many students learn very well in classrooms where they do not particularly even like the teacher. If students are convinced that a teacher has their best interests at heart, they will tolerate all manner of personality flaws on the part of that teacher.

A good rapport with your students is among

the greatest assets you can have as a teacher. It will save you from a multitude of problems over the course of a year. Because of this you must work diligently to establish and maintain a good relationship with your students. Always remember that you will only teach a student if you first reach the student. Any effort to reverse this order is an exercise in futility.

Cliché #2:
Nothing is taught
until something is learned.

This is a good sentiment for teachers to keep in the forefront of their thinking because it helps to keep them honest in assessing their own effectiveness. Teachers are judged by their ability to teach. The only effective indicator of this ability is the degree to which their students have learned. If students can show concrete, tangible evidence that they have mastered a given subject, then their teacher can be sure he did an effective job. Conversely, if there is no tangible evidence of student achievement, the teacher still has a great deal of work to do.

This becomes a frustration for teachers when they come across those students who simply do not learn in their classes. Sometime during your career, you will come across students who will not benefit from your efforts to teach them. They may try harder than any students you have ever had, or they may not try at all. Regardless, you will find no evidence that they have learned anything from you. If you find yourself in this situation, your obligation is to keep trying simply because nothing is taught until something is learned.

The temptation in such a circumstance is to place some or all of the blame on the student. To do so is to compromise your integrity. The education of your students is, first and foremost, your responsibility. Therefore, if they remain uneducated, it is primarily your fault. This does not mean that you will be able to teach every student who walks into your classroom. It means only that you are obligated to try and to keep trying. Sooner or later you will encounter students who will thwart your best efforts. At the end of the year, if they remain unchanged, uneducated, and unimpressed, add them to what should be a very short list of your personal failures and move on. If you admit your limitations and defeats, you will be better equipped to overcome them. You will also be empowered to serve the vast majority of students who you will find yourself able to reach. If you blame it on the students, you will only become bitter. It is your fault. Get over it and get back to work.

Cliché #3:
New teachers shouldn't smile
until Christmas.

This would only be true if the first two clichés were false. Since the first two are true, this sentiment should be ignored completely. Without a doubt, the most important thing teachers must do before anything can be accomplished in their classrooms is to develop good relationships with their students. To do this, teachers must show their students that they are compassionate human beings. Human beings smile. It is one of their nicer characteristics. Therefore, you will need to smile too, and long before Christmas.

There is a kernel of truth within the original sentiment. Fortunately, veteran teachers usually make such statements with tongue planted firmly in cheek. There is wisdom to be found in taking the substance of this warning seriously even as you recognize the cliché as an overstatement. You will cause yourself great difficulty if you are unable to convey an air of seriousness to your students. As the new kid on the block, you will be viewed differently than teachers with whom students are more familiar. They will try repeatedly to make you show signs of weakness. Specifically, they will try to make you take your job less seriously than you should. If they succeed, or even if they think they have succeeded, you will spend the rest of the school year battling to keep your students on task. Class time will be one long, continuous effort on your part to keep your students from going off on a tangent. Rather than focusing on the work to be done, you will be waging a war to maintain time on task. This is a losing proposition for everyone.

Therefore, you would be wise to be very guarded in your approach with your classes. Never get too relaxed too soon. Establish the standard of what you expect from your students right away. Remember that in terms of discipline it is always easier to relax your grip on a class that is under control than it is to tighten the reigns on a class that has gone wild.

Does this mean you should frown through November? No. In every class there is room for laughter, joking and frivolity. Just make sure the students are laughing with you and not at you. Establish high standards for your students and then have as much fun with them as possible. In rare cases you may wish to remain more reserved, but in most classes you should smile on the first day and keep smiling throughout the year. Unless of course you find yourself teaching a class of nineteen-year-old freshmen. In that case, don't smile until Easter.

Foundation Stones for Building Good Rapport with Your Students

Since a good relationship between student and teacher is essential for true learning to take place, it is important at this point to look at the principles which serve as the foundation of such a relationship. These principles provide support for everything a teacher does in the classroom. If they are firmly established and in place, then every opportunity for success remains available to the teacher. If one or more are missing, a teacher will be hard-pressed to establish any kind of quality relationship with his students. With this in mind, every teacher should make an effort to live according to these standards and to establish classroom guidelines which complement them.

Principle #1:
Everyone is looking for a good community.

Human beings exist in a relational world. In order to survive, they must interact with both their environment and their neighbors. It is simply human nature to desire that this interaction be as pleasant an experience as possible. People tend to thrive in circumstances which make them feel comfortable and secure. They tend to struggle in situations where they feel out of control. In order to ensure his students' success, a teacher must provide a setting within the classroom that maximizes opportunities for students to achieve. This will be most likely to occur if he is able to convince his students that the class in which they are enrolled is a good community.

The establishment of a good community is vital for success in teaching. Before teachers are able to teach anything, they first need to establish a dynamic that allows a class to be more than just a collection of individuals. To be sure, students enter a classroom as individuals, yet they are taught as a group. At some point the teacher will need to address the reality that from the many must come one. To do this he must build a good community.

A good community can take on many forms, but at its core it must serve the needs of each individual without jeopardizing the welfare of the group. Teachers, therefore, must build an environment in which students feel that they are receiving individualized instruction and also feel that they are contributing to the common good. Students should leave a class each day feeling they learned but also that they made the class better because of their participation. In this case, the students' desires for the class are not that much different than your own.

Principle #2
You can delegate authority, but not responsibility.

One of the most effective ways of building rapport with your students is to let them have a say in the day to day operation of the class. Students who feel they have a voice in their own education tend to be more motivated than students who do not. It is in your best interest to empower your students as much as possible in this regard. To accomplish this, you should delegate some of the decision making to your students. As they show themselves adept at handling responsibility, you should delegate authority in increasing measure.

Consider the idea that students in any class should always be given the right to accelerate the pace of their learning. While a teacher may have planned to cover a given topic during a two week period, there is no educationally sound reason for prolonging instruction if students master the concepts in a shorter period of time. If students achieve in one week what their instructor thought would take them two, there must be some way available for moving the class forward. Certainly the decision to do so could be made by the teacher, but there is no reason why it could not also be made by the students. A good teacher will always provide the opportunity for his students to express their desire to proceed with the learning process. In so doing, he delegates authority to his students in an appropriate and effective way.

In such a scenario, the teacher must always remember that he is the expert in the classroom, not his students. Therefore, while he can delegate authority, he must acknowledge his absolute responsibility when it comes to ensuring a positive outcome. Should students think that they are capable of moving forward to new material, the conscientious teacher will allow them the opportunity to prove themselves in this regard. Should they fail in this endeavor, it remains the sole responsibility of the teacher to develop and implement a solution to the problem at hand. Good teachers allow their students to reach for success. Should the same students fail in their attempts, however, it is the good teacher who also has a way to help them overcome their difficulties.

Principle #3
Love makes up for a multitude of sins.

In helping students to overcome their difficulties, teachers demonstrate love, compassion and understanding to the youngsters in their care. This is a vital aspect of any good relationship you will have with your students. You have already learned that students' response to your direction will correspond with their belief that you have their best interest at heart. They truly will not care how much you know if they are convinced that you do not care. Therefore, expressing a sincere love and appreciation for your students is a necessary component of any effort to establish a good working relationship within your classroom.

Ironically, the best opportunity you will have for demonstrating such concern for your students will come when they are in the process of enduring their greatest failures. At some point during the school year, each of your students will struggle through some aspect of life in your class. Whether this struggle manifests itself in the area of academics, behavior problems, or inadequate social skills is insignificant. What matters is that you work diligently to help the students through their difficulties. As they search for the good community described earlier, students are often most concerned with how their mistakes will be handled. If they realize that the response to their mistakes will be nurturance and guidance, the class will soon become the good community for which they are searching.

Principle #4
Tough love makes up for even more.

There is no more difficult task in teaching than administering appropriate discipline in the classroom when things go wrong. To get this job done, sometimes you must employ tough love. The reason for this is simple. Students are not adults. They do not have the requisite maturity to make appropriate decisions in every circumstance. Sooner or later their adolescent behavior will cause a conflict which you must address. You must address the behavior simply because it has caused a disruption in the good community you previously established within the classroom. When a student displays inappropriate behavior in a classroom, the effects are immediate and wide-spread. Not only does the misbehaving student diminish his own ability to learn and profit from the class, he limits the opportunity of others. Just to maintain a sense of order and fairness, a teacher must correct the behavior and ensure that it will not be repeated.

This is by no means an easy task. Quite often, teachers faced with handling a difficult student must put aside their own anger before they can make any positive strides toward rectifying the situation. Any honest veteran teacher will confess that there have been times when mis-behaving students have caused thoughts of restoration and reconciliation to be far outweighed by thoughts of revenge and retribution. Yet such thoughts do not lead to loving discipline; they lead to punishment. They are also counterproductive. The goal of the classroom teacher, in terms of classroom management, is to establish an environment where discipline is respected rather than rejected. To this end, any teacher entering the classroom should remember . . .

Principle #5
It is better to install sprinklers than to fight fires.

The teacher who has a well-conceived plan for classroom management avoids all manner of problems. Truth be told, there are few areas of concern you should focus on more before entering the classroom. Whether you like it or not, you will eventually encounter difficulties in your class. It is vital that you know how you will respond before the problem arrives. Just as the sprinkler activates when exposed to heat, your response to difficulties in your class should be automatic. To be sure, there will be problems you can not anticipate, but teachers who consider their response to classroom problems ahead of time are far more effective educators than those who make up their plans as they go.

What follows are twelve specific suggestions for maintaining a positive environment for learning in your classroom. It is by no means an exhaustive list but provides enough information for you to establish good rapport with your students and practice effective classroom management. As you progress in your career, you may develop a different list. On the other hand, there may be enough collected wisdom here to carry you through to retirement. What matters is not what techniques you use to manage your classroom but rather that you have a plan in the first place.

Practical Techniques for Building Good Rapport with Students

1. Plan until you can't plan any more.

Ask any veteran teacher and he will tell you that the days when the most things go wrong are also the days for which he is least prepared. If you are looking for the simplest way to avoid problems as a teacher, make planning a priority. Much like an actor is well-versed in acting, a teacher is well-versed in teaching. Yet neither can be successful without a script. No matter how well you know your material, you will be unable to present it effectively without first developing a detailed plan for your presentation. So plan! Begin with the big picture and work toward the small. You should enter your classroom every day with a detailed outline of what you will do and how long it will take you to do it. Vary the techniques you employ so students will maintain their focus and interest. Approximate how much time you will spend on each activity. Anticipate potential problems and develop ideas on how to resolve them. Bring your lesson plan for the following day as well. It will give you something to do if your initial lesson runs shorter than expected. Most importantly, remember that there is no way that you can plan too much. Even if you could, it would get you into far less trouble than planning too little.

2. Establish clear and comprehensible guidelines.

Many people think that students push against the limits imposed by authority because they desire to have those boundaries removed. To the contrary, students push against boundaries because they want the boundaries to be well-defined. This is human nature. If this does not sound right to you, consider the fact that every year millions of people step to the edge of the Grand Canyon. Yet no one in his right mind would do so on a dark and moonless night! There is great freedom in knowing where the boundaries are. When people know what is expected of them, they tend to feel more at ease. They also are more willing to rise to a high level of expectation.

As a teacher, you must establish clear and comprehensible guidelines for your students. Early in the school year, explain the reasons for the existence of your rules, and the logic behind them. Tell your students what you expect of them and why. By defining the boundaries in this way, you will be giving your students the freedom to move within the structure of your class without taking unnecessary risks. Keep expectations simple, but make them clear.

3. Be consistent.

Having established clear guidelines for the day to day operation of your class, you could not make a more deadly mistake than to be inconsistent in employing them. Once you have established the parameters which will govern your class, you must employ all diligence to abide by them. If you do, you will model positive behavior that your students will emulate. If you do not, you will have lost their respect permanently.

4. Model excellence.

If you expect excellence from your students, you must first model excellence in your profession. To do less would be to practice hypocrisy. Students will only respect a rigorous standard you set for them if they first see that you apply it to yourself. Each day your students should see you put forth your best effort on their behalf. The classroom should be appropriately prepared for their arrival. Materials that you provide should be neat and organized; free from spelling mistakes and grammatical errors. Presentation of the daily lesson should be crisp, effective, and eloquent. You are the teacher. If you expect excellence, you must teach excellence. Does this mean you have no margin for error? No. It means only that glaring mistakes on your part should be the exception rather than the rule.

5. Know your students and yourself.

There is no doubt that children of all ages can prove to be frustrating sometimes. Perhaps this is so because children have such a profound ability to expose the faults in the adults around them. If you teach for long, you will probably begin to wonder if your students have a sixth sense or a special hormone that allows them to spot hypocrisy whenever they see it. Kids are adept at exposing discrepancies in what they see.

For this reason alone, it is important that you know both your students and yourself very well. Find out what they like and what they do not like. Find out what really bothers them. At the same time, recognize your own limitations and faults. Trust begins with honesty. The teacher who is honest with his students will find that they are honest with him. There is no better foundation for building a relationship.

6. Know when to say when.

No matter how well you succeed in building a good working relationship with your students, there will be times when your students will need you to cut them some slack. Like any other relationship you have, the one with your students will need room to breathe. It is one thing to push students to higher levels of achievement, it is quite another to push them beyond what they can bear. With this is mind, be conscious of the fact that you will sometimes need to let your students relax.

Often this is a function of timing. Certain times of the year are more stressful to students than others. Certain times are more fatiguing as well. The good teacher is cognizant of this fact and plans accordingly. Never push your students on the day before Christmas vacation. Likewise, when they seem to be trying but can not quite grasp the material at hand, give them a five minute break to regroup. Knowing when to slow down or provide rest for students is among the hardest lessons for a beginning teacher to learn. There must be a balance in your approach, for it is far too easy to develop a habit of wasting class time. For this reason, many new teachers fear giving their students any down time at all. Yet in the long run they must. No child will be able to maintain a high level of attention and dedication throughout an entire school year. Eventually, your students will need the freedom to disengage from the learning process in order to return to it later with renewed zeal. As a good teacher, you must recognize this and make sure it happens in the right way and at the right time. An ineffective teacher will struggle forward and force the issue. This is the equivalent of kicking students when they are down. It is a sure-fire way to make enemies and should be avoided at all costs. Push your students until they bend, not until they break.

7. Establish tradition.

Students entering a class at the beginning of the school year should immediately get the impression that they are becoming part of something larger than themselves. The most effective way to ensure this is to establish class traditions. The student who participates in a class with strong traditions knows that those who came before him helped shape the reality he now enjoys. He also knows he will help shape the future for those students who follow in his footsteps. This serves to provide students with a sense of both identity and purpose. Both are valuable assets for the classroom teacher who wishes to instill a sense of pride in each and every student.

In addition, classes which have a long standing history of traditions gain a reputation within the school as worthwhile places to be. This serves to heighten the level of anticipation present in students who enroll in the class. A heightened level of anticipation serves to make the traditions grow even stronger, and the cycle continues. When students enter your class on the first day and ask questions regarding whether or not the traditions will continue, you will know you have arrived. You will also have the added advantage of having extra leverage when it comes to keeping students well behaved and under control. Students who show respect for an established tradition will in no way want to jeopardize its future. Whether it be an annual field trip, a student talent show, or a canned food drive, a well-established tradition will serve to keep both you and your students focused on a common goal.

8. Command respect.

Anyone can demand respect, but a successful teacher must command respect. No matter what strategies a teacher employs in an attempt to build a good classroom dynamic, if there is no respect from the students, it has simply been a waste of time. Respect is the cornerstone of any solid foundation within the classroom.

How can you command respect? By making sure you never do the things that would cause you to lose it. Never raise your voice to talk over an unruly class. It shows you lack control. Never embarrass a student. It shows you lack empathy and compassion. Never expect less of your students than they are capable of doing. It shows you lack integrity. Most importantly, never allow your students to think that anyone other than you has the final decision-making authority regarding what happens in your classroom. If you do, your students will quickly realize that, when it comes to respect, you are demanding what you cannot command. You could be in no worse position as a classroom teacher.

9. Instill fear.

Fear is a great motivator. It is also a great equalizer. Significantly, it is not always bad. Although it sounds negative, it is important for teachers to be able to instill fear in their students.

The more important thing, however, is that the fear itself is well-placed.

Fear with an improper focus is destructive. This is not the type of fear you want. Your students should not be afraid of you, nor should they be afraid of failure. Such fear is unhealthy. Instead, the fear you should instill in your students involves the program you are running in your classroom and its associated work ethic. In simplest terms, you want your students to believe that you have something to offer that they dare not miss. Make your class compelling. Teach it with revolutionary zeal. If you convince your students that you hold the keys to their future success, they will be afraid to miss out on the lessons you offer. This is precisely the kind of fear you want.

10. Walk a mile in their shoes.

If there is one belief which is universal among children, it is the belief that adults do not understand them. "Generation gap" is among the most accurate and descriptive phrases in the English language. You will go a long way toward establishing rapport with your students if you can show them that you are different in this regard. Get to know your students and try your best to understand them. If you are unable to understand them, at least show them you are willing to make the effort. Sometimes the attempt is just as important as the desired result.

There are a thousand ways to get to know

your students but the best way involves going through experiences with them. When students realize that you are willing to walk with them as they face the difficulties of a typical school day, you will immediately win their affection, respect and loyalty. Do everything you can to see life through their eyes. Eat lunch in the cafeteria. Sit in the student section at football games. Attend school dances. Dance! In whatever way you can, let your students know that you are making every effort to understand what their lives mean to them. When you realize the impact this has on your relationship with your students, you will consider it time well spent.

11. Open your life.

Just as it is important for you to understand the things your students face, it is important for them to understand the life you lead as well. This does not mean that you should spend inordinate amounts of class time sharing intimate details of your home life. Rather, it means that you should let your students know a bit about who you are. Be sure to tell every class what makes you happy as a teacher. Weave personal experiences into the design of your lessons. Tell your students good stories about your best moments and your worst. Explain to them your hopes and dreams for the future. In so doing, you will reveal to them your humanity. This is a good first step in building any relationship.

12. Make full use of calculated insanity.

Finally, only one strategy remains for building a good rapport with your students and a positive environment in which to work. Make full use of calculated insanity. Never let your students know what might come next. Always keep them guessing. If you can, convince them that (in the most positive of ways) you might just be a little bit crazy. The teacher whose students never know what to expect is the same teacher who has their undivided attention. He is also the teacher who has the most fun. So join that kickball game at recess! Play in the faculty-student basketball game. Have the school's most unique costume on Halloween. Enjoy yourself and your students will enjoy you too.

Some Final Thoughts Regarding Classroom Management

Classroom management and the building of relationships with students dominate the thinking of new and veteran teachers alike. No matter how long a teaching career lasts, the one thing on which every teacher can count is the fact that there will always be a need to find constructive ways to work with students. There can be no teaching without someone who is first willing to learn.

While it would be nice to assume that all

students enter every class with a strong desire to perform and succeed, this is simply not the case. Most students, in fact, depend upon their teachers to instill in them the guidance, direction and desire necessary for their success. In this battle to develop an appropriate work ethic in their students, all teachers interact with a common set of variables: parents, students, colleagues, and administrators. What is important for teachers to realize is that each of these groups can be for them a great asset or a great liability.

Parents who are convinced that their child's teacher is both knowledgeable and wise will support the teacher's efforts in every way they can. Students will respond in a similar manner. Colleagues who are persuaded that a teacher is truly committed to pursuing excellence in teaching will soon become a valuable source of support and insight. Likewise, administrators who feel that a teacher is working diligently to improve the quality of the school will aid that teacher in any way possible.

On the other hand, parents, students, colleagues, and administrators can become formidable liabilities for the teacher they feel is not living up to their standards of excellence. It is in your best interest to make allies rather than enemies. Contact parents early in the year. Make sure this first contact is strictly positive. Talk to your students one on one and let them know you are concerned for their welfare. Demonstrate your commitment to your colleagues and supervisors. You have much work to do.

Even if you employ each of the suggestions made in this chapter, there will still be days during your school year when things go sour. From time to time, you will return home at the end of a long day and feel as miserable about your job as any human being on earth. On average you can count on ten horrible days per year. They will come no matter what you do. This is both a harsh

reality and your saving grace. When all else fails and you have had a terrible day despite your best efforts, remember the ten day rule. After a disastrous day at school, return home, put your feet up, circle the date on your calendar and enjoy the rest of your evening. After all, there are only nine bad days to go!

Chapter 7
Planning for Success
Methods of Effective Lesson Planning

During the first years of my teaching career, I had the unique privilege of working with a genius. His name was Dan and he taught students physics and engineering. Over the course of his illustrious career, he and his students turned a converted stock room into a fully equipped engineering lab. Working within the lab, they developed a wide variety of ideas, receiving patents for their inventions in the process. Eventually, in what became Dan's favorite project, they designed and built an airplane from scratch. Without a doubt, Dan was a man of keen intellect and motivational skill. Yet Dan's teaching ability was only a part of what made him a genius. As a teacher he was the best in the school. As a human being he was among the most fascinating people I have ever met.

My first encounter with Dan took place early in my first year of teaching. At the time, I was only two months removed from college and about as green as a rookie teacher could be. As if this point needed to be emphasized, I found myself working in a department where eight of the nine teachers had more than twenty years of teaching experience. Needless to say, it was a year in which I learned some very humbling lessons. Joining me in this experience was my new boss, Angela. With only six months experience as an assistant principal, she found herself the new supervisor of our school's science department. This placed her in the unenviable position of trying to convince eight veteran male teachers that her ways were best.

On this particular day, Angela had scheduled an "advisory meeting" to be held with the science department members immediately after school in the room of our department chair, Lou. The topic of the meeting was lesson planning and each of us was required to bring our lesson plan books for her to review. As each of the nine men of the science department reluctantly trudged through the door at the end of the day, the atmosphere was filled with both tension and fatigue. Lou sat at his teacher's desk, not having bothered to move after the day's final bell. Spread before him were nine student desks turned to form a circle. Each of us slid into one of the desks until only two remained empty, one beside Lou, and one beside me. Angela entered the room, glanced at the configuration and sat down beside Lou. Thirty seconds later, Dan entered the room and lowered his rail-thin six-foot-five frame into the seat next to mine.

Despite her attempts to appear otherwise, Angela was clearly nervous. The meeting got off to a rocky start as she explained her belief that any department composed of veteran teachers might eventually get sloppy or lazy in lesson planning and therefore needed to be monitored carefully by a qualified administrator such as herself. Around the room, hair began to rise on the back of each man's neck. Yet each man said nothing, patiently waiting as Angela continued to place her foot in her mouth, and then watching with satisfaction as she proceeded to swallow it whole. As I watched the process unfold, I became keenly aware of the cause of their resentment. These were outstanding teachers who knew what the classroom required. They also understood the value and necessity of quality lesson planning. To be reminded of it through a condescending lecture from an inexperienced administrator was more than they desired to endure, especially at the end of a long day.

Sensing the growing agitation in the room, Angela decided to talk less and act more. Not wanting to appear as if she had lost control of the situation, she turned to Lou and in her most authoritative voice asked to see his lesson plans. With a stare that could melt glass, Lou slid his lesson plan book along his desk toward Angela, allowing it to come to rest just beyond her grasp. Awkwardly, Angela half rose from her seat and reached for the book. Unable to maintain her balance in such a strained position, she fell heavily back into her chair. Around her, several teachers fought back a smile.

Opening Lou's plan book, Angela placed her reading glasses on the tip of her nose and began professorially scanning the pages. After only a few seconds she lowered her glasses to the table, having never taken her hand from them.

"I can't read these," she announced.

Unfazed, Lou reached out to take his plan book from her outstretched hand. "Just another reason I'll never ask you to teach my classes," he replied.

In an instant Angela had lost the battle of wills unfolding before me. What followed was a conflict that grew more intense with each passing minute. Unwilling to retreat from her original position, Angela continued to review the lesson plans of each science teacher while the rest of us reluctantly watched. In each case she found some reason to deem the lesson plans unacceptable and each time she was rebutted by a science department that was becoming increasingly bold in its questioning of her credibility. As the time approached for my plan book to come under scrutiny I felt a distinct sinking feeling in the pit of my stomach. Like it or not, I was caught between the proverbial rock and hard place. Would my colleagues expect me to challenge Angela as they had? As the new kid on the block, I did not want to appear unsure of myself in front of my fellow teachers. On the other hand, I also had no desire to alienate my new boss. Self-consciously looking down at my plan book, I was convinced that things could not possibly get worse. I was wrong.

With only a few weeks of teaching experience, my knowledge of lesson planning techniques was limited to what I had learned in college. I wrote lesson plans exactly as I had been taught. They were letter perfect, textbook quality, and totally unrealistic. Much to my chagrin, this was exactly what Angela wanted. Handing my plan book to her, I sat back in my seat and awaited the harsh words of her inevitable critique. Instead, a smile began to form on her face. Then, as I tried in vain to think of a place to hide, she proceeded to explain to eight teachers with over 200 years of combined teaching experience why they should follow the example of someone who had been at it for six weeks. Silently, I wondered if I would ever be able to work with these men again.

Then Dan came to my rescue.

Returning my plan book and congratulating me for my outstanding effort, Angela looked toward the one teacher whose plans she had yet to review.

"Dan, did you bring your plan book?"

As if awakened from a daydream, Dan startled to attention.

"What?"

"Your plan book. Did you bring it?"

That Angela would even ask this question was a recognition of Dan's genius. No one else had been given the courtesy of being asked whether he had brought his plans. For us it was a given. It was expected. Dan, however, was given a little leeway. In recognition of his singular abilities, Angela and the rest of the administration were more than willing to make allowances when Dan did not fit the conventional mold. Because the rest of the staff also recognized his ability, none of us ever seemed to mind either.

Slowly, Dan responded to Angela's query. Shifting his unlit cigar from one side of his mouth to the other, he moved his long, angular limbs and raised himself from his familiar slouch to a more upright position in his chair. Looking as if his mind remained elsewhere, Dan leaned forward and moved his hand toward his back pocket. Frowning, he then reached for his other back pocket. With a growing look of concern, Dan began moving his hands slowly about his body, patting each of his pockets as if searching for a lost set of keys. Finally, as he reached his right hand to the breast pocket of his shirt, a look of recognition and relief came over his face. Reaching inside the pocket, Dan pulled out a wrinkled 3 x 5 index card with one corner torn off. Handing it to me, he motioned for me to pass it around the circle to Angela. Five words were scribbled across the back of the card.

"What's this?" Angela asked, spinning the card slowly in front of her face.

"Lesson plans," Dan replied proudly.

Lowering the card to her desk, Angela looked incredulously at Dan.

"There's only five words written here."

"Right," Dan replied, "one for each class."

"That's all you plan for your five classes?"

Biting hard on his cigar, Dan smiled broadly.

"Yep."

Around the room, smiles crossed the faces of the other science teachers. Trying not to laugh, they looked straight down, eyes fixed on the floor beneath them. For the first time since the meeting began, Angela appeared unsure of what to say. Looking down at the card, she stammered a final question.

"What happened to the corner?"

All eyes turned to Dan. His brow furrowed; it appeared that he was deep in thought regarding the question. Holding the card, which had by now been passed back to him, he stared thoughtfully at the torn corner. A look of recognition once again came over his face. Rising from his desk as if to signal the end of the meeting, he turned toward the door and offered his explanation.

"One of my kids needed me to write him a bathroom pass."

* * *

If you are a genius like Dan, five scribbled words on a torn index card will provide more than enough planning for you to be a successful teacher. If you are not a genius, however, you will need to come up with another method. It is worthwhile to look at the planning process as it relates to quality teaching. Good planning makes for good teaching, yet becoming an effective lesson designer is one of the most difficult things for a new teacher to do. Somewhere between the extremes of writing five words on a card or writing lesson plans that read like a Russian novel lies a balanced approach that will allow you to be an effective lesson planner. Finding that balance is the focus of this chapter.

How to Find a Balanced Approach for Lesson Planning

Remember that lesson planning will occupy much of your time as a new teacher. As you become more experienced as an educator, you will also become more efficient and more adept at the lesson planning process. In the beginning, you will gain wisdom only by spending long hours mastering this aspect of your craft. Since experience is the only way to validate your ideas, you will learn each of your lessons through the process of trial and error. With this in mind, consider two points that will help to keep you focused on the task at hand.

Point #1:
Your lesson planning work load will expand in direct proportion to the amount of time you allow for it.

This is simply another way of saying that there is no limit to the amount of time you could spend planning lessons. This is true because there is basically no way that you can be too prepared for the classroom. The more prepared you are, the better you will be. Yet there is a point of diminishing returns associated with the lesson planning process. You can spend hours refining the details of a lesson without seeing any appreciable result. Eventually, the continued effort you put forth in preparing yourself for a given lesson starts to offer little or no benefit in return. The key is to avoid wasting time. Many (if not all) new teachers make the mistake of spending valuable time working on things that will prove superfluous once class time begins. If you find yourself spending hours adding fine points to your lessons, details that only you will notice, it is time to reduce the amount of effort you devote to lesson planning. As a general rule, no lesson should take longer to plan than it does to execute. When it comes to lesson planning, avoid beating a dead horse.

Point #2:
Lesson plans are only as effective as the lesson that follows them.

While you certainly do not want to overdo the lesson planning process, it is equally important to remember not to cut it short. After all, the ultimate aim of lesson planning is success in the classroom. Lesson plans are good only if they lead to successful lessons. An effective teacher always views revision as a key component of the planning process.

Your lesson planning process should involve a minimum of three steps: brainstorming, refining, and revision. By brainstorming, you will establish the "big picture" idea of what your lesson will look like and how it will be executed. Once you have established this picture in your mind, ideas regarding how you will actually conduct the lesson must then be refined and completely developed. This will provide you with enough information to carry out the lesson in the classroom, yet the lesson planning process is far from done. Once the lesson is taught, you must also evaluate its success and revise any weak aspects the lesson has. By doing this, you continue the process of perfecting your lesson planning technique. Since your goal is to teach effectively for many years, you would be wise to maintain this mindset throughout your career. By developing and continually refining your lessons, you will maintain your commitment to excellent teaching and become a credit to your profession. Always remember that there is room for improvement within any of the lessons you teach, and that the success of any lesson is determined by the answer to only one question: Did it work?

Planning Effective Lessons

When a teacher sits down to develop an effective lesson, her thoughts must begin with a simple question: What is the point? In answering this one question, a teacher takes the most important step toward guaranteeing her own success. By determining the ultimate goal of her lesson, she defines not only what she will teach, but how she will teach it and what its eventual effect will be. Therefore, anyone wishing to be an excellent teacher should begin the lesson planning process here.

Yet even veteran teachers make the mistake of skipping this all-important first step. Rather than examine the ultimate goal of the lesson, they begin instead with questions of what they will teach and how they will teach it. This is a mistake of the highest order. By beginning with a question regarding ultimate intent, a teacher is able to give clear focus to the lesson's design. Without this focus, a teacher is building without a foundation and the best possible results will never be realized. As mentioned previously, nothing is taught until something is learned. Therefore, the ultimate point of any lesson should revolve around what the students of the class will learn. This is the point! If you find yourself unable to define the ultimate goal of a lesson, look closely at what you want your students to learn. If your lesson design offers no indications that they will learn anything, you can be sure it is ill-conceived and should be revised.

As an example, consider an English teacher who wishes to give her students an appreciation of the poetry of Robert Frost. If she skips the first step of the lesson planning process, she will find herself designing lessons that focus strictly on content alone. When asked what she is teaching her students, she will reply "Robert Frost." Yet what does this mean? Will she teach her students to recite Frost's poetry? Will she detail the cultural circumstances which influenced his writing?

Will she ask them to write poetry of their own? Undoubtedly, the potential exists for her to do all of these. Yet if she does not begin by articulating the ultimate intention of her lesson, she will never know what mark to hit. Rather than aiming for a well-defined bullseye, she will find herself hoping a target appears after she has taken her best shot.

If instead she begins by asking, "What is the point?" she will provide an avenue by which she can teach her students exactly what she wants. If her ultimate intention is to help her students appreciate the depth of Robert Frost's work, she can employ a wide variety of strategies to reach her goal. Most importantly, she will know when she has accomplished it. By beginning the lesson planning process with this simple question, she has guaranteed the best chance of success in the classroom. She has accomplished each of the important steps in designing quality instruction, establishing clear direction for both herself and her students while at the same time developing a framework within which instruction will be accomplished. In terms of providing clear parameters regarding how instruction should take place, this one little question makes all the difference.

Types of Lessons

Establishing the "big picture" or "ultimate intention" of your lesson provides an overview of where you want to take your students. It does not, however, get them there. In a very real sense, all you accomplish with this first step of the planning process is to provide yourself with a "bird's eye view" of your educational strategy. Just as cartographers rely on aerial photography in order to construct accurate maps, professional educators rely on their ability to develop a "big picture" view of what they wish their classes to be. What remains lacking is detail. Having established your direction, it is time to work out the nuts and bolts.

As an aide to your lesson planning endeavors, remember to consider the process involved in your lessons as well as the content. By doing so, you move beyond the "what" of your lessons, and focus on the "how." There are a thousand ways to accomplish your goals as an educator. What you, as a professional, must decide is which one of them is the best for your particular group of students. It is just as important to determine what your students will do as it is to determine what they will study. For this reason, it is sometimes useful to consider the types of lessons you can employ when teaching.

In terms of lessons, each effort made by a teacher to educate her students can be categorized according to the lesson's purpose. The most typical lesson is the lesson that presents new and meaningful information to the students. Since a basic goal of all education is to teach students something they do not already know, teachers are constantly in need of methods that will allow them to share relevant information with their students. This will be the type of lesson with which you most commonly work. However, the successful presentation of course material is often dependent upon a teacher's ability to utilize other types of lessons which do not present new material. Among these are lessons which prepare students for new learning, as well as lessons which allow students to process or practice with the information they have received. These types of lessons play vital roles in allowing students to achieve depth in their learning. Rather than taking information into their short-term memory only, students taught with a wide variety of lesson types are able to develop their ability to maintain and expand upon what they have learned.

Finally, some lessons are evaluative in nature. In these lessons, students are given the opportunity to show what they have learned. This is a fundamental part of any good teaching program because students must be given the opportunity to apply what they have learned before it will have any lasting value in their lives. If they are never given the chance to use their new knowledge, it will soon be considered irrelevant and forgotten. Even if your lesson plan for the day involves nothing but a test, that lesson plays a crucial role in the effective functioning of your class. When developing the strategies you will employ in teaching your students, remember to provide opportunity for each of the lessons described here:

Lessons that PRESENT new material.

Lessons that PREPARE students for future learning.

Lessons that allow students to PROCESS course material.

Lessons that allow for student PRACTICE, and

EVALUATIVE lessons that allow students to show what they have learned.

The Nuts and Bolts of Lesson Planning

Where should you start? How can you make your creative teaching ideas a reality in the classroom? After all, much of what has been discussed so far is philosophical rather than practical. How should you go about making the rubber hit the road?

For the sake of simplicity, you should begin with a calendar. Timing is crucial in education, so it should be the first place to start. Work from large time units to small, beginning with the entire school year and working your way down to individual lessons for specific days. Along the way, consider plans for marking periods, months, and weeks. Do everything in your power to avoid planning lessons the day before they occur. As a lesson planner, you should go about your business in much the same way a tourist would plan a long trip. A traveler planning a lengthy excursion would begin with the general and work toward the specific. You should do the same. A school year is like a journey. It should be planned accordingly. In keeping with this analogy, consider the following time intervals and how they should be addressed.

Planning the School Year

In planning for the entire school year, you are making the same types of decisions a traveler makes when choosing his destination. Just as a traveler might choose to visit Phoenix, Orlando, or Chicago, you are choosing the stops you would like to make during the academic year. The key questions at this stage of planning are: Where do you want to go? and Why? When deciding where you want to go, you are basically deciding what you wish your students to become during their time in your class. This should be done in the broadest terms possible. It should also be limited to a few concise, clearly defined objectives for your students to achieve. At this level the focus is on process, not content.

For example, an English teacher may decide he wants his students to become better writers. Or a math teacher may wish for her students to become effective problem solvers. In each case, the goal is clear, concise, generic and attainable. The result is a clear picture in the mind of the teacher regarding what he or she wants to attain. All that remains to be developed is a broad-based timeline for achieving the goals. For the English teacher who wishes to improve his students' writing skills, such a timeline can be developed by using just a small number of mileposts. Since the teacher wants to determine if his students have improved, he must first know where they stand in terms of writing ability. Making this determination could be the focus of the first marking period. During the second marking period, he can help his students identify strengths and weaknesses in their writing and so on. Finally, at year's end, the teacher can compare his students' current writing with the efforts they made at the beginning of the year. Then, and only then, can he make an accurate assessment regarding the overall success of his teaching effort for the year.

While it may seem that such broad spectrum planning is too generic to be of much practical use, consider what happens if it is neglected. If a teacher does not take the time to establish clear, year-long goals for himself and his students, how will he know if he has accomplished anything as a teacher during the course of the year? He may be well-aware of his students' success with a particular unit of study, but he will have no idea how they were changed by participating in his class. While he does run the risk of failing to achieve his goals, at least he will know what he has done. Without such goals, he will be unsure of whether he has accomplished anything. Having aimed at nothing, he will undoubtedly have hit it.

Planning for the Marking Period

Marking periods are artificial time units used only in schools. Most schools have four per year. Some have five. Apart from providing struggling students with the opportunity to start over, the most useful aspect of the marking period involves planning lessons.

Since marking periods break the school year into more digestible portions, they also provide convenient mileposts for teachers planning their educational programs. To understand how this works, consider once again our intrepid traveler who has finally decided on Phoenix as his final destination. Having chosen Phoenix as the city he wishes to visit, he must now decide what he wishes to see and do when he arrives. To begin this process he might divide his possibilities into broad categories. Does he wish to attend sporting events or would he rather explore museums of Southwestern art? Do the natural wonders of the area intrigue him or is he more interested in the city's nightlife? These are the questions which will shape his itinerary and determine what his experience in Phoenix will be. This is much the same process a teacher goes through in planning for a marking period. Having established the big picture view of what the year-long goals are, a teacher can use a marking period plan to put in place the steps that will lead to success in achieving those goals. To be successful in planning for a marking period, ask yourself what experiences you would like your students to have during that time. Again, the focus here remains on process rather than content.   Specifically, what will you have your students do during the marking period in question that will help them achieve your goals for the year? When you have an answer to this question you are ready to begin . . .

Planning for the Month

Monthly plans mark the boundary between planning for process and planning for content. They are also the first plans to exist for someone's benefit other than your own. Monthly plans may be reviewed by your supervisor; because of this, they require a higher degree of formality than yearly or quarterly plans. Not only will monthly plans serve as a guide to where you are going with your students, they will serve as a record of where you have been. When you update and revise lesson plans for the following year, it will be monthly lesson plans that provide the focal point for your efforts.

It is important to identify the characteristics of effective monthly plans. Among these, the most easily overlooked is the fact that quality monthly plans must be psychologically effective. Unlike marking periods, months are not artificial time units constructed only for schools. Instead, they are artificial time units recognized as useful by the entire culture. An effective teacher will take advantage of this to give her students an unspoken sense that time is moving forward and progress is being made. To accomplish this, monthly lesson plans should have a distinct beginning and a distinct end. As much as possible, these milestones should correspond with the turning of the calendar page. A teacher wishing to develop monthly plans should begin by asking how much course-related material she can cover during the month in question. She can then begin her month by telling her students what material is soon to come their way. At month's end, she can say with confidence, "This marks the end of this unit of study." Students will be cognizant of a page turning in their educational experience; with a sense of both completion and anticipation, they will be ready to move forward.

Accurately judging the amount of time a unit of study requires will be a very difficult thing for you to do as a new teacher. Because of this, developing monthly lesson plans may prove frustrating. It is important to remain focused on the most vital characteristic of monthly lesson plans. Monthly lesson plans must have a high degree of linearity. One lesson must flow into the next lesson, which must in turn flow into the next. There must be a tangible, logical pattern in the sequence of lessons you establish. Like a path through a forest, your monthly plan must lead your students to the desired destination. Sometimes the path may turn to the left or the right, but there can be no doubt in your students' minds that there is a path. Monthly lesson plans allow both you and your students to realize that you really do know where you are going.

The only question that remains is: What happens when a month's worth of lessons takes longer than a month? This will undoubtedly happen to you during your first year. Since you have never planned instruction for an entire school year, you will most likely underestimate the amount of time it will take for you to cover material in your classes. This need not be a major concern. What is important is that students are provided an opportunity to mark progress during the course of the year. If these mileposts happen to match up with the dates on a calendar, that is an added blessing. If they do not, it is the marking of progress that counts, not the time at which it occurs. There is nothing wrong with ending September's monthly plan on October 15th. In fact, this can work to your advantage by reminding students that they are progressing at a rate slower than you anticipated. If you find yourself in this circumstance, make a point to acknowledge the completion of your unit of study and then move on! After all, the next month's plan awaits. How will you accomplish it? Week by week.

Planning for the Week

It is in planning for a week's worth of instruction that you must move past the single word descriptors found on Dan's index card. Weekly plans must be neat, organized, coherent and detailed. You are at this point putting meat on the bones of the skeleton you have already established with your yearly, quarterly, and monthly plans.

As a starting point, commit to memory the most important (and ironic) rule of weekly lesson planning. NEVER PLAN FOR ONLY ONE WEEK! If you do, you will find the instruction you deliver to be choppy and inconsistent. Arriving at Friday afternoon having completed your list of things to accomplish for the week, you will be hard-pressed to pick up where you left off once Monday rolls around. Because you will have built into your week a stopping point for your thoughts, you will find yourself unable to reestablish the frame of mind that lead to your original lesson design. As a result, your lessons will lack continuity from one week to the next. If, on the other hand, you remain one week ahead in your thought process, you will achieve the linear flow outlined in your monthly plan. As a general rule, when you enter school on Monday, you should know not only what you plan to teach during that week, but also what you plan to teach during the following week.

This leads us to the (equally ironic) second rule of weekly lesson planning. NEVER PLAN MORE THAN TWO WEEKS AHEAD! If you do, you will find yourself constantly revising and replanning because of changing circumstances within your classroom. With so many variables involved in the teaching process, there is no effective way to anticipate what will be happening more than two weeks in the future. Will your students understand the material you are currently teaching? Will they cover it in less time than you expect? Until the actual teaching takes place, there is no way to know. It is pointless to try to prognosticate regarding your students' long term performance. As a happy medium, planning for this week and next is an effective approach.

When it comes to the actual development of weekly lesson plans, form should follow function. Since the purpose of weekly lesson plans is to provide an overview of a two week learning cycle, begin the process by deciding what topics you will cover in class on each day of the two week period. Then determine what activities will allow for the best coverage of this material. Write your plans in outline form or the equivalent with no less than one week of plans per page. This will allow you to list the strategies you plan to employ beneath the topics you intend to cover, with the resulting document allowing you to view two weeks of instruction at a glance.

Planning for One Day

Developing daily lesson plans to be carried out in the classroom is a process as unique to a given teacher as his own teaching style. There is no "correct" way of writing daily lesson plans. What matters to you as a teacher is whether or not they work. It is imperative that you develop a method of lesson planning that works for you. A good lesson plan is one which allows you to deliver instruction effectively. Whatever works best is what you should do.

While developing yearly, quarterly, monthly, or weekly plans is comparable to the many levels of making travel arrangements, successful daily lesson planning necessitates a different type of approach. To effectively develop a lesson plan for a given block of instruction, you must think like a script writer rather than a tourist. This is the case because script writing is exactly what you are doing when you develop a single lesson plan. Sitting down to write a plan for teaching a class involves envisioning all that will take place once the class begins. Just as a script writer anticipates what will happen in a scene from a movie or a play, you must visualize what will happen on the day you deliver your lesson. Develop a short but poignant introduction which will grab your students' attention. Follow this with a clear deliniation of what you intend to achieve during the class. Continue with a sequence of activities that will allow your students to absorb the material in a number of different ways. For each activity, make sure your students have something to do (listen, write, sketch, etc.) and something to ponder (concepts, applications, problems to solve, etc.). Finally, provide closure for your students by developing a culminating activity for the lesson that will allow them to review the material covered while looking forward to what comes next. As a visual representation of what you are trying to develop, consider a spiral or a spring. Each loop doubles back to overlap one that came before, yet the overall structure of a spiral moves from one place to another. This is exactly what you are doing when you teach. Each day of teaching involves reminding your students of what they now know, introducing new material, and focusing their minds on what is to come. Such an approach ties students' learning to their past, present, and future. In this way learning becomes relevant and meaningful.

Relevant and meaningful learning is the primary goal of all education. Your lesson plans should reflect this truth accordingly.

Chapter 8
An Orange for the Teacher
Non-Traditional Teaching Methods

If you have ever pruned a rose bush, you could handle an orange clipper. Today, however, you would be lucky to even find one. While there is little difference between an orange clipper and the shears used for pruning roses, an expert could tell the difference --- an expert on citrus farming that is. Even among citrus farmers, there are fewer each year who are knowledgeable about the workings of an orange clipper. It has simply been too long since the clippers played any major role in the industry. This was not always the case.

Orange clippers were once the tool of choice for every citrus farmer in the country. Every worker in the fields carried a pair. When picking time came, it was an orange clipper in the hand of a skillful worker that took the oranges from the trees. The same was true for tangerines, but no one talked of tangerine clippers. While tangerines were a tasty fruit, oranges were the cash crop. Farmers knew what kept food on their table.

Yet there would never have been orange clippers were it not for tangerines. Tangerines plug. In laymen's terms this means they fall apart if you try to pick them off the tree without clipping. If you pull a tangerine from its perch on a tree, a chunk of skin and fruit will remain on the branch. In your hand you will hold a piece of fruit, perfect in every way but for the large "plug" ripped from its center. As a result of "plugging," tangerines are never "picked" from trees in the way an apple would be. Instead, they are clipped just above the point where the fruit attaches to the branch. For over fifty years, oranges were clipped in the same way.

Then an interesting thing happened. As citrus farms spread through both Florida and California, a process was developed that would revolutionize the industry: Frozen concentrate.

What frozen concentrate provided for citrus farmers was the equivalent of a brand new market. By allowing them to process some of their crop in a way that prevented spoiling, farmers were no longer forced to sell all their fruit fresh. Instead, some of their fruit could be processed and stored to be sold at a later date. In addition, fruit that was not attractive enough to sell as produce could be processed and sold for juice. No one cared how ugly a juice orange was once it had been turned into concentrate.

But the story does not end here.

In the years that followed the development of the frozen concentrate process, citrus farmers enjoyed unprecedented success. Because they were able to ship their product worldwide at low cost, it seemed there was no limit to the growth potential for the entire industry. Then came the big freeze.

It was one of the coldest spells in years. In Florida, conservative estimates stated that seventy percent of the crop would be lost. Once again, the makers of frozen concentrate came to the rescue. "Get us your oranges within three days and we'll make them into juice," they said. So the owners of Florida's citrus farms filled their groves with local and migrant farm workers. Each was provided with a ladder and a bushel basket. None were given orange clippers. In their haste to get the oranges to market, they discovered an interesting thing. Oranges don't plug; they come off the branch without a blemish. Fifty plus years of clipping oranges from their trees had all been wasted motion. Somehow, nobody had ever thought to check.

Before you shake your head in wonder that anyone could operate for so long under what turned out to be a wrong assumption, keep in mind that public education has done the same thing numerous times. An objective look at the history of American education shows many cases where that which was best for the students was ignored for the sake of tradition. The wheels of change spin very slowly in the world of public education.

As an example, consider the case of a Florida high school principal. Upon his transfer to a new school, he decided to "walk through" the registration line in order to get a feel for what his students would face. At each station along the way, he asked the person in charge to explain the purpose of his particular part of the process. No purpose could be found for seven of the twenty-five steps! Written registration cards that had long been replaced by computer entries were still being completed. Insurance forms which did not apply to the students in question were still being distributed. The needs of the system had changed, but no one had bothered to update the process. They simply continued to do what they had always done. Tradition stood in the way of progress.

* * *

In the world of public education, progress is a cyclical process. The predominant school of thought in education today will also be the dominant view in twenty to thirty years. In the interim, however, an opposing view will rise to prominence, achieve a fair degree of success, and then fade away to the dark recesses of educational theory, waiting in exile for its return to power.

Progress in public education can be likened to the actions of teenagers from years past who spent many an hour wearing deep grooves into the surface of their favorite forty-fives. While these items were purchased as "singles," they invariably contained two pieces of recorded music. When the "hit tune that would never grow old" did just that, the "B side" would be explored for all its artistic worth. Since this was often a work of less artistic merit, it usually received less playing time; even so, it afforded the opportunity for an alternative when that which had been so new and innovative became old and a bit monotonous.

Likewise, public education in the United States has held a long-standing tradition of alternating between dichotomous approaches to educating the nation's youth. Switching to the "B side" seems to occur about every twenty years. More often than not, the paradigms associated with the opposing sides center themselves around the debate over the validity of traditional and non-traditional methodologies. The argument manifests itself in a variety of forms such as: phonics versus whole-language, closed versus open classrooms, and the debate over classical versus vocational education.

In a very real way, the cyclical nature of public education is a function of the creativity of the people who compose the system. Teachers, by their very nature, are people who need to be creative; they have an inherent desire to try things that are new to them. Because of this, there will always be a voice within the educational community championing the cause of that methodology which is not currently in vogue. "Progress" occurs for educators at the point when the educational approach which has been lying fallow gains enough supporters to be considered viable once more. The fact that implementing such an approach is not innovation as much as it is regurgitation is lost to everyone except those educators who have endured long enough to see the cycle repeat several times.

This flip-flopping within the educational community would be insignificant were it not for the fact that, while they are typically flexible, teachers are extremely intolerant of teaching methods which do not work. Therefore, since these opposing ideologies continue to exchange places along the cutting edge of educational theory, it can only be assumed that each possesses a certain degree of validity. Were this not the case, the non-traditional approach (side B) would not continue to receive the playing time it does every twenty years or so.

The questions for you as a new teacher are: Which type of teaching methods, traditional or non-traditional, will be best for you? Will you employ the textbook and lecture approach characteristic of traditional education or will your students learn through cooperative learning and other non-traditional methods? As you answer these questions, keep three important things in mind. First, remember that the traditional approach to education exists for a good reason. The traditional approach is "traditional" simply because it has stood the test of time and been effective for a large number of teachers. As an educational philosophy, it has the advantage of being widely accepted and recognized, while allowing its proponents a great deal of flexibility. In addition, it is highly effective. Otherwise, it would not have endured the challenge of the classroom for this long. While many new teachers equate "traditional" with "boring," this is not necessarily the case. Under the direction of a highly skilled teacher, a traditional lecture can be one of the best lessons taught.

The second item to remember is that you, over time, will develop your own educational

traditions. As you gain experience in the classroom, you will find that some lessons are so
successful that you will want to use them every
year. By default these lessons will become
traditional. What was new and innovative during
your first year will not be once you have taught it
ten years in a row. This does not mean it will have
become ineffective. Instead it will have become a
refined, artistic, model lesson -- battle tested, tried
and true.

Finally, you must remember that the most
effective and engaging classrooms are those which
employ both traditional and non-traditional
approaches to teaching. As the saying goes, variety is the spice of life. The teacher's corollary?
Monotony is the kiss of death. With this in mind,
the question at hand becomes one of when to use
each type of approach in your classroom.

Traditional vs. Non-traditional Teaching Methods

When should you employ a non-traditional
approach to teaching your students? Whenever it
will work better than a traditional approach.
Traditional methods should be employed whenever non-traditional methods offer no additional
benefit. In teaching there is no need to reinvent
the wheel, only to make sure the tire is inflated.
You should use what will work best. Never lose
sight of the question that brought you here: What
is the point?

A caveat is in order here. If you choose a non-traditional approach simply for the sake of trying something different, you are probably headed for disaster. Without a sound educational reason for employing them, non-traditional approaches tend to sink like the proverbial lead balloon. In the meantime, they require far more preparation than traditional methods, thus putting you in a position of double jeopardy. Not only will you have spent hours of preparation time in developing your lesson, you will also find it to be generally ineffective. Rather than minimizing your energy loss, you will have created a great deal of work for no appreciable result.

Here are several non-traditional methods of teaching that you may wish to try. In each case, the benefits and burdens of the given strategy are listed along with circumstances under which it would be effective.   The list is by no means exhaustive, but it is intended to provide you with an idea of the possibilities.

INQUIRY

Inquiry is a non-traditional method originally developed for the teaching of science. Made famous by the BSCS Biology, ChemStudy and PSSC Physics programs developed during the post-Sputnik years of the late fifties and early sixties, the inquiry method champions the idea of students making their own discoveries in science rather than having a teacher do so for them. At its best, inquiry allows a student to "do" science rather than just learn "about" science.

To develop an inquiry lesson, a teacher must first determine what it is she wishes her students to learn. Having done so, she can then begin developing a sequence of activities that lead her students to the "discovery" of the appropriate concept.

As an example, consider the classic lesson offered at the beginning of the ChemStudy program. In this lesson, the goal is to show students how important it is to observe accurately and to make good assumptions based on their observations. The lesson itself simply involves students watching a candle burn. While this may sound like a simple activity, it becomes a dramatic learning tool in the hands of a gifted inquiry teacher. Having supplied candles and matches to her students, the teacher also provides a set of clearly defined tasks, usually in written form, which guide the students through their learning. These tasks begin with the simple request to list ten things the students observe while watching the candle burn. As this process takes place, the effective inquiry teacher circulates throughout the room, encouraging her students to make their observations as specific as possible. For example, an observation that "the flame is yellow" could be refined to "the flame is multi-colored, yellow near the top, orange and red near the middle, and blue near its base." To accomplish this refining, the teacher could simply respond to the original observation by asking, "Is it really yellow all the way through?" As the students explain that the flame is not in fact actually yellow, their teacher can direct them to refine their observation until it accurately represents what they see.

While it may not seem that much science can be learned by observing a burning candle, an important occurence soon takes place that makes the exercise worthwhile. Without even realizing it, students invariably switch from observing to inferring. They recognize the need to provide an explanation for what they see. Soon statements of "observation" begin containing the word "because." An observational statement such as "the flame is shaped like a cone" is soon enhanced with the phrase "because rising heat pushes it into this shape." Without prompting, students have moved on to the next logical step in the scientific process: hypothesizing. The options for the teacher at this point are limitless. If she forces her students to eliminate explanations from their statements of observation, she develops in her students an ability to make bias free observations. Should she decide to leave the statements of explanation in place, she gains the opportunity to challenge her students' explanations and teach them how to develop a good hypothesis. Ultimately, the teacher can provide the greatest challenge to her students by asking them to offer proof that their explanations are accurate. If challenged appropriately, students will be conducting experiments before they leave the classroom. By allowing her students to do science rather than just hear about it, she has lead them through all the component parts of the scientific process before class has ended on the first day.

This is the greatest strength of inquiry: it provides great opportunity for students to gain large amounts of insight in a very short period of time. In the example shown, a teacher of chemistry is able to cover the workings of the scientific method in a day. Similar content coverage using a traditional approach might take a week.

Economy of time in the classroom does not come without a price. While they allow students to grasp concepts quickly and accurately, inquiry lessons are inherently difficult to develop. Having determined what it is that you wish your students to learn, you must then develop a fool-proof sequence of activities and events that will lead them to the appropriate conclusion. This is by no means an easy task. Anticipation is the key. If you are able to anticipate what your students will do in response to the direction you provide, then you will be able to develop effective inquiry lessons. Remember that no matter what you do in terms of preparation, your students will find a way to mess it up. Some of your students will come to the wrong conclusions. This is part of the risk involved. Remember also that developing an inquiry lesson plan from scratch requires hours and hours of work. Your students will get it quickly because you, as their teacher, got it slowly.

To be a successful inquiry teacher, you will have to let the learning process run its natural course. Whether you like it or not, you will need to keep your mouth shut. You will need to allow your students to make mistakes even when you could easily prevent them from being made. Most importantly, you will need to be willing to start from scratch if the whole process goes sour.

Inquiry is not for everyone. Since it requires hours of advanced planning to develop inquiry lesson plans, many teachers reject it as a viable alternative for everyday use. For them it simply requires too much time. Because of this, "canned" inquiry packages continue to be made available by a variety of curriculum publishers. Researched and tested, these packages allow teachers to take advantage of the many strong points of the inquiry approach without having to deal with its chief liability.

This is true not only for science teachers, but for a wide range of educators. As a teaching method, inquiry has expanded far beyond its original target audience — the sciences. Inquiry has become attractive to teachers in a variety of disciplines and can be used to teach everything from mathematics to multiculturalism. As is typical, quality educators have shown that a successful teaching method, in the hands of a dedicated professional, can be used to teach almost anything.

Your level of success in using the inquiry method depends as much on your temperment as any other factor. As stated earlier, inquiry is not for everyone. Because it is unpredictable and difficult to control, the inquiry method takes many teachers beyond their comfort zone. There is a definite risk involved in employing the method.

Students are likely to draw the wrong conclusions from their efforts and many teachers do not feel this is good practice. Much like a speculative investment, inquiry offers high risk along with its potentially high reward. If you are not a person who would willingly take such a risk, inquiry is probably not for you.

Why take such a risk? Because the lessons learned through the inquiry approach are lessons remembered for a lifetime. Although the risk can be great, the reward can be greater. For many teachers, this is enough of a benefit to make the gamble worthwhile. The opportunity to teach multiple concepts in a single day outweighs the risk involved. If the inquiry fails, these teachers are still several days ahead of the game. For them, inquiry plays a role similar to the proverbial girl with the curl in the middle of her forehead. When it is good, it is very, very good. When it is bad, it is horrid. If you can live with such a reality, find an appropriate inquiry lesson that someone else has written and try it yourself. You will know right away if inquiry is for you.

ALTERNATIVE ASSESSMENT

Every teacher gives tests but not all tests are created equal. This is the basic principle behind alternative assessment.

As the name suggests, alternative assessment involves assessing things in a different way. Before attempting an alternative assessment, it is important to realize that the difference lies in the method, not in the content, of the assessment. Wrong answers are still wrong. Right answers are still right. What changes when an alternative assessment technique is employed is the manner in which students are able to deliver their answers.

There are a thousand different ways to use assessment in the classroom. What determines the effectiveness of a given alternative assessment is the same thing that drives any decision to use a non-traditional teaching method. Does it offer a clear benefit over more traditional methods? If it does, you may want to consider using it.

Some methods of alternative assessment have been used so frequently they are becoming traditional in their own right. Books have been written regarding how to use portfolios, develop rubrics, and the like. Rather than focus on individual types of alternative assessment, examine the underlying principles associated with the process. When considering an alternative assessment strategy, the most important thing for you to decide is what you want your students to understand. This is the driving force behind any successful assessment, alternative or otherwise. If you are unsure or unclear regarding what you want your students to learn, you will be unable to assess their success no matter what method you employ.

As an example of how to employ an alternative assessment strategy, consider an art teacher who wishes to give her students an appreciation of

art history. Having introduced her students to a
wide variety of art works and styles, all that
remains for the teacher to do is assess her
students' level of understanding. If her efforts
have been successful, her students will be able to
show an understanding of composition and perspective as they demonstrate an ability to distinguish between various art movements. How best
can she allow them to show what they know?
Using conventional techniques of assessment, the
teacher would have her students complete a quiz,
a test, or perhaps a report. Yet none of these
methods truly assess the knowledge desired.

As an alternative, the teacher could give
her students the opportunity to interact with art
more directly. By providing her students with
reproductions of art works through slides or
photographs, the teacher could have her students
develop an "art show" of their own making. By
choosing a collection of their own and then
presenting it to their fellow classmates, students
are able to show their understanding of art in a
realistic and tangible way.

CONTRACT GRADING

For years teachers have been trying to
convince their students that school is preparing
them for the "real world." With this in mind, many
teachers have decided to drive this message home
with a little more force. They have removed from
their classrooms the conventional assessment

techniques associated with schools and replaced them with an outside world alternative. Rather than maintain the traditional structure of tests, quizzes, and grade point averages, these teachers have chosen to employ something with which students will inevitably need to become acquainted: a contract. The principle which drives the contract grading method is simple. Since the teachers who employ it all work under a contract which determines their job responsibilities, they assume their students might as well do the same.

Contract grading works this way: Students are responsible for learning the material associated with a class just as they would be in any other course. What changes is the way they are asked to process their learning and provide feedback to their teachers. At the beginning of each term, students sign a "contract" which details their responsibilities for the duration of the marking period. In addition to deliniating what students must do during the marking period, the contract also explains how they will be graded. At the end of the marking period, grading involves only a simple determination of how well the students fulfilled the parameters of the contract.

For example, consider students who take a math course which employs contract grading. At the beginning of the term they are given a contract by their teacher which details five tasks they must complete. During the marking period they must:

1) Accurately solve 100 problems from the textbook.

2) Pass at least two tests with a grade above 80%.

3) Teach the rest of the class one twenty-minute lesson on a topic to be assigned by the teacher.

4) Solve one "brain bender" challenge problem.

5) Complete 75% of the homework.

Notice that the structure of the contract provides flexibility for both the teacher and the student. Students are required to complete 100 problems, but the teacher will probably assign more. Students are given the freedom to pick and choose. Because of this, students are given the freedom to miss some of the problems without adversely affecting their grades. In a similar way, the homework requirement allows for the occassional night off should the student have a family commitment or other conflict. For the teacher, the work load associated with grading is greatly reduced because the burden of proof regarding what has been accomplish during the term falls squarely on the students' shoulders. At the end of the marking period, the teacher need only count up how many of the tasks a student has completed in order to determine his grade. This assessment can easily be made through brief conferences with students, during which they show what work they have completed. Not only does the contract help in the teaching of math, it also teaches responsibility. Because each student will ultimately need to present his work to his teacher, he must remain diligent and organized throughout the term. These are skills which will serve students well throughout their working lives.

Because the teacher is required to evaluate his students' performance, the contract must also provide a method for the teacher to determine a numerical or letter grade. In this regard, contracts provide the simplest grading method available. The final decision regarding whether all tasks have been successfully completed belongs to the teacher. Determining final grades becomes a matter of simply filling in a checklist. For the teacher of our hypothetical math class, students who complete all five tasks receive an "A," students who complete four of five tasks receive a "B," and so on. Grading with the contract is no more difficult than counting to five.

If you are thinking of employing a contract based grading system, you should consider two things. First, you should realize that the benefits associated with contract grading far outweigh the burdens. Contracts tend to motivate students, simplify grading, reduce paperwork, and provide real world experience for students. With this in mind, there hardly seems a reason not to employ it. However, the reason not to employ contract grading is the most important thing for you to consider. In this regard, the second point is far more significant than the first. Contract grading will only work in certain, special and specific circumstances. If you attempt to employ it elsewhere, you are destined for failure.

Contract grading will only work in an environment where students have reached the highest degree of either maturity or desperation. Therefore, it must be employed with great care. For those students who have typically been successful in the conventional classroom, contract grading is put to its best use when they have reached the highest level course offered within their school. Contract grading works wonderfully with high school seniors, for example. Having proven themselves responsible during their years as underclassmen, contract grading provides a welcome alternative to the normal method of grading. Since they have reached the highest level of maturity, contract grading provides them with the level of respect and freedom they feel they deserve.

Contract grading also works well with those students who have been unable to achieve success through any of the conventional routes. For these individuals, contract grading provides a fresh start and new hope. Rather than repeat their failures by doing poorly on quizzes, tests, and the like, these students often thrive when given the chance to take their learning into their own hands. Because of this, contracts are often employed by many "second chance" schools. For the right student in the right circumstance, contract grading is the best non-traditional teaching method that will ever exist.

THINK TANKS & CLASSROOM CORPORATIONS

In keeping with the notion that exposing students to real world situations is a good thing, many teachers across the country have adopted the strategy of forming think tanks or corporations within their classes. The idea behind this approach is simple. Since students will eventually need to have their ideas stand the test of the marketplace, why not give them that opportunity while they are still in school?

When it comes right down to it, there are literally dozens of ways to accomplish this. For teachers who choose to employ the think tank strategy, the driving force behind their coursework is the idea that students should solve actual, real world problems rather than those that are fabricated for classroom use. Therefore, teachers who employ this technique must commit themselves to providing opportunities for their students to work outside the confines of the classroom. Problems for students to solve can come from any number of sources within the community. Government classes can examine the difficulties faced by local planning boards or zoning officers. Science classes can work with local engineering firms to analyze solutions to a neighborhood construction problem. No matter where the challenge is found, the key is to get students thinking about questions that community members actually need to answer. In ideal circumstances, students just might be the ones who develop the idea that no one else considered. In doing so, they learn that viable ideas are valuable no matter what the source. As examples of success, consider the sixth grade student who saved valuable wetlands from development by demonstrating their ecological worth to his town council, or the eighth grade student who saved the National Park Service thousands of dollars each year by suggesting they turn picnic tables upside down each fall in order to avoid damage from crushing winter snows. Some of the best ideas in the country are found among our youth. Teachers who turn their classes into think tanks allow those ideas to blossom and grow, benefitting all of us.

Teachers who turn their classrooms into corporations take a similar approach. The idea here is that students are fully capable of producing a product that would be considered viable in the open market. While the purpose of such an approach is not to turn a profit, there is still much to be learned in the process of trying to run a class like a business. Even though monetary gain is not the ultimate goal of this technique, there are still countless examples of how classes have achieved dramatic success in marketing a product or idea.

As perhaps the best example of how this can work, consider the story of history teachers within the school system of Rabun County, Georgia. Faced with the challenge of teaching local history to high school students, these teachers realized that their best resource was the untapped oral history available among the older residents of the county. Within the mountains of the area lived dozens of "oldtimers" who held vivid memories of mountain life before there was electricity, telephone, or indoor plumbing. Seeing the rich resource available to their students right in their own backyard, these teachers sent their students out to conduct interviews of people who remembered life in the mountains before the turn of the last century. Armed with tape recorders, notebooks, and cameras, these students documented rich traditions of the mountain people of northern Georgia which would otherwise have been lost. The result of their efforts was later published as the "Foxfire" series of books which won numerous awards. Proceeds from the sale of the books later built the Foxfire Museum. Students continue their research to this day. Check out some of their work at your local library and you will easily see the value of this approach to education.

PAPERLESS CLASSROOMS

Perhaps the next non-traditional technique to work its way into classrooms across the country will find its roots in the emerging technologies that are so rapidly changing the world as we know it. With the advent of Internet technologies and advanced computer capabilities, it is possible that we will soon see the first truly paperless classroom. Since digital technologies are so prevalent, is it possible that the student of tomorrow will enter a classroom with no books, no handouts, and no need for paper-based assignments? It is quite possible. More significantly, it is just as possible that students of the future may not even need to come to class at all. Through the wonders of virtual reality, the class might come to them. Will it someday be possible for a student from Indiana and another student from New York to attend class at the Parthenon without ever leaving the comfort of their homes? No one knows. Yet there is one thing of which you can be sure. If a resource becomes available to teachers in the future, they will surely find a way to use it. Perhaps you will be among those leading the way.

Chapter 9

Grunt Work!
Paperwork and Other Misfortune

From an actual job description for a teacher in a moderately large, regional school district in New Jersey . . .

"With regard to routine duties, teachers will maintain appropriate and accurate records. They will submit written lesson plans which contain clear-cut objectives, sufficient detail, and specific reference to course proficiencies. Teachers will make efficient use of instructional time. They will demonstrate performance of institutional duties and compliance with district policies, procedures and timelines. They will accurately provide for the monitoring of student progress and growth, while simultaneously showing an ability to maintain discipline and student control.

In terms of organization and planning, teachers will prepare for instruction by developing short and long-term plans which include objectives, activities, and varied techniques and assignments which reflect continuity and course proficiencies. They will demonstrate an ability to effectively use class time by presenting instruction with clarity and by addressing individual student abilities. Teachers will employ instructional techniques that use various materials, strategies and resources to foster participation, stimulate critical thinking and verify student understanding. They will evaluate the progress of each individual student using multiple evaluation techniques and will design instruction based on student performance.

With regard to human relations, teachers will interact effectively with students, staff, and community, fostering an environment that is conducive to learning, mutual respect of individual and cultural differences and open communication. They will display and encourage empathy and sensitivity to individual needs and concerns. They will promote self-efficacy by providing opportunities for success. Also, teachers will resolve conflicts and encourage positive interaction and behavior. If applicable, they will identify and refer students in need of assistance to appropriate specialists.

Finally, teachers will demonstrate initiative and creativity by seeking and incorporating innovative teaching techniques, strategies, and resources which guide students into successful learning experiences. They will foster divergent thinking and initiative in students, encouraging them to develop alternative solutions to problems. Teachers will show initiative toward personal and professional growth and contribute to district curriculum development activities . . .

. . . plus any other tasks deemed necessary by the administration."

Among the things that will prove surprising to you during your first year as an educator is the significant amount of time you will need to spend doing work that has no effect on your teaching. Student teaching does not prepare you for this. Neither does your wildest imagination. There is simply more work to do than you ever could have conceived.

Undoubtedly, you thought your student teaching experience was overwhelming. If your experience was typical, you taught classes all day, planned lessons all night, and graded papers when you should have been sleeping. Surely, you thought, it must get easier. In truth, it does, just not yet. Your first year of teaching will prove just as overwhelming as student teaching was, and for good reason. This year you will have to learn to live with grunt work.

Whether you realized it or not, the educator who lead you through student teaching protected you from grunt work. Although you remained profoundly busy during your time as an apprentice, you most likely were not exposed to the full set of responsibilities facing a classroom teacher. The administration probably never asked for your help on a project. You were undoubtedly not a member of the faculty advisory committee or the board for attendance appeals. There was good reason for this. You did not know what you were doing. That is why you were a student teacher; your directing teacher and the rest of the staff and administrators knew your abilities were limited. Therefore, you were left alone regarding grunt work.

Grunt work is to teaching what scraping is to painting a house. It is tedious, thankless work. It is not satisfying in the least, yet it is absolutely essential. If you faithfully complete your grunt work, you are guaranteed no additional success in the classroom, but if you ignore it you can count on trouble arriving before long. Taking attendance, grading papers, attending meetings, and completing paperwork all constitute grunt work. So do many other tasks you will be asked to complete. It will take hours of your time and it will offer little direct benefit for your teaching. Grunt work is simply one of education's necessary evils. You will need to do it well if you wish to be a success.

To be successful in completing your grunt work, you must realize that while it rarely adds anything to your teaching, it has the potential to be a major liability. Because of this, it is vital that you remember the most important principle provided in this book: Teaching selects toward those individuals who minimize an energy loss. Before teachers can achieve excellence in their profession, they must first learn to survive the rigors of the job itself. Those who cannot minimize their energy loss will find themselves unable to keep afloat in the flood of responsibilities. Remember that you must guarantee your survival within the profession before you can consider the quality of the job you are doing. No educator can say he has done a truly excellent job if he is unable to complete it. Like a race car driver, to finish first you must first finish.

The focus of this chapter is the reduction of

your energy loss while performing education's most mundane tasks. If energy loss can be minimized here, it will mean you have more energy available for the classroom. More energy in the classroom will make you a more effective teacher. Becoming a more effective teacher is the first step on the road to professional excellence, and professional excellence is your ultimate goal.

Grading Papers

In an ideal world, there would be no need for students to complete assignments. In such a world, students would learn each of their lessons on the first try and would have no need for practice or repetition. Unfortunately, this is not the world you will find in your classroom. Students do not always learn material on their first attempt. They need practice. They need reinforcement. This means they need to complete assignments. It also means that you will have papers to grade. At first glance, grading papers seems like an easy task. For new teachers there is even a little bit of thrill associated with wielding the all-powerful red pen. Yet as soon as the novelty wears off, paper grading is revealed for what it really is: a time-consuming, tedious process.

The reality of paper grading begins to settle in the first time a new teacher realizes how much time it requires. A little math clarifies this point instantly. If a teacher has a typical teaching load of 120 students (5 classes with 24 students in each), he will have a corresponding number of papers to grade after giving an assignment. If he takes only one minute to grade each paper, he will still need two full hours to get his students' papers marked. This does not include the recording of grades (in a gradebook or on a computer) which must follow. If he gives only two assignments per week, he can count on spending at least five hours performing tasks related to grading.

It is easy to see why grading papers runs the risk of being a major energy drain for any teacher. To avoid this, there are a few key principles that every teacher should employ while grading in order to minimize an energy loss.

1. Keep it simple.

Considering the time commitment associated with correcting assignments, there can be no better advice regarding grading than to keep it simple. You can do this in any number of ways. As a starting point, consider the way you will determine your students' grades at the end of a marking period. When all is said and done, their final grade will be derived from a combination of assignments such as quizzes, tests, homework, reports, etc. Undoubtedly, some of these assignments will be of greater importance than others. As a result, you will want the important assignments to play a more significant role in determining their final grade. What to do?

For starters, you should determine the

simplest way to assign a grade for each assignment. If you are numerically inclined, you could give assignments a score such as 85 points out of a possible 100. If you are a traditionalist, you could simply call this a "B." Having established a grade for each assignment, you are still faced with a problem. How will the individual grades for each assignment combine to give one comprehensive marking period grade? How will each assignment be provided an appropriate "weight" in determining this final grade?

If you are committed to making your life easier, you will construct a grading system that does most of your work for you. If you believe tests should prove more significant than homework, then score them accordingly. Make tests worth 100 points while homework assignments score only 20. Make quizzes worth half as much as tests. In doing so, you will automatically provide appropriate weighting to each assignment and will need only divide points earned by points possible to determine each student's grade. As an approach to grading, there are few systems that are simpler, and when it comes to grading, simplicity is best. Whatever grading system you develop, keep simplicity in mind. With numbers, add and divide. Never subtract and never multiply. It only serves to muddy the water. If you find yourself spending long hours with a calculator, or if the eraser is always worn off your pencil, you have made things too complicated. Rethink your approach and try again.

2. Have a reason for every assignment.

In the old days this was known as having a method to your madness. The same question that serves as the foundation for lesson planning also applies here. What is the point? Before giving your students an assignment that you will eventually grade, you must ask yourself this question. Every assignment should have an academically sound reason for its existence. Students who complete the assignment successfully should find themselves more enlightened than they were previously. Class assignments should enhance the learning experience of the students who complete them.

Your purpose in giving assignments can vary. At times, you will want simply to evaluate your students' level of understanding. At other times you will want to provide them with practice as they learn a difficult concept. Whatever your reason, the important thing is that you actually do have a reason. Students are quick to recognize assignments that have no academic validity. They even give such assignments a special name: "Busy work." Avoid such assignments at all cost. Your students will hate doing them, and you will hate grading them. Why waste everyone's time?

3. Know your destination before beginning.

Having sworn off busy work, you will need to become adept at developing effective, high quality assignments. As you do this, be sure to always keep the ultimate end in sight. Never give an assignment without knowing how you will grade it.

This may sound like a simple point to make, but it is often an area that causes problems for new teachers. Stretched to the limit by his intense work load, a new teacher might not feel he has the time to develop a twenty question multiple choice test. A five question essay test would be much easier to develop and as a result becomes his evaluation of choice. Yet how will he grade it? What criteria will he use in developing his answer key? If he is not careful, he may find himself distributing the test to his students long before he has considered the answers to these questions. He will place himself in the unenviable position of having to formulate grading criteria that match his students' answers rather than having their answers match his pre-established standard. He will also have lost all objectivity and credibility associated with the assignment.

To avoid this predicament, a teacher must always remember that when it comes to developing assignments, form follows function. Know what you desire of your students before you go looking for it. Make sure your assignments match your goals. If you desire to have your students articulate the depth of their thoughts regarding a given subject, then an essay assignment is appropriate. If instead you are looking to test their knowledge of factual information, an objective evaluation may be in order. Whatever your intended outcome is for an assignment, the form of the assignment should allow you to achieve your goal. Also, students benefit from knowing the "rules" of the assignment beforehand.

In addition to allowing you to accomplish your goal, an effective assignment will also allow you to get the job done easily. Therefore, you should make your assignments "grading friendly." Set up your assignments in such a way that you will have no problems grading them. For example, if your students are solving math problems, make them draw boxes around their answers. This will allow you to focus immediately on what is important and will prevent you from having to search aimlessly through an entire page of calculations. Simple techniques like this are guaranteed time savers. Look to employ them wherever you can, remembering always that if the time taken to grade a paper is reduced from one minute to 30 seconds, your two hours of work suddenly becomes only one.

Theory Into Practice

Take time to brainstorm timesaving ideas for your subject area or grade.

4. Use tools effectively.

There are dozens of tools you can use in the process of grading. Among these, the computer is your most valuable asset. Suppliers of educational materials offer countless grade book programs that provide an easy way for teachers to chart their students' progress. While these programs vary in quality, they all have at least one thing in common. They save time. Using a computer to calculate grades is the only efficient way for a new teacher to conduct business. Get yourself up to speed as soon as possible.

For another grading tool, consider the use of an abbreviation sheet. Abbreviation sheets have been employed by teachers in a wide range of subject areas. The concept behind an abbreviation sheet is a simple one. Why write an entire word (or sentence) when a few letters will do? What makes abbreviation sheets valuable is the time they save in those circumstances where you might find yourself writing the same directive over and over. If, for example, you find your students making the same error on a given assignment, you can save valuable time in grading if you employ an abbreviation sheet system. The system works this way. First, grade one set of papers from a class, taking the time to develop a detailed list of all the mistakes made by your students. Then, give each mistake a three letter code. Run-on sentences become "RUN." Disjointed writing becomes "DSJ." You are then able to return the papers along with a list of mistakes and corresponding codes.

Students can then refer to the abbreviation sheet in order to determine what they need to correct or improve. The abbreviation sheet becomes for the students a handy reference for understanding your analysis of their work. For all future assignments, you can identify any error on a student paper by simply writing three letters. As they become familiar with the system, students will know exactly what they did wrong without your having to write an explanation for them. Three letters tell them everything they need to know, and new codes can be added to the list as needed. (See example)

Sample Abbreviation Sheet Entries:

Code	Description of Problem
DSJ	Disjointed writing style.
EXP	This explanation is incomplete or incorrect.
RON	Ronald Reagan Writing: You start every sentence with "well."
RUN	This is a run-on sentence.
WWD	This is the wrong word to use in this context.

Theory Into Practice

Write out positive comments. While it may be tempting to utilize an abbreviation sheet for both negative and positive feedback, it is in your students' best interest for you to write detailed explanations of what they have done correctly. This strategy, combined with the use of an abbreviation sheet, allows you to give your students an appropriate context for your feedback. Positive results are identified as things worth considering, while negative results are shown for what they are: simple stumbling blocks to be corrected and overcome.

5. Speak softly and carry a big stick.

One final area of concern regarding grading is the potential for conflict with students who do not agree with their grades. This can be a major cause of stress for any teacher, but is especially troublesome for new teachers. To avoid this stress, there are some simple steps you can take that will minimize your chances of entering a prolonged battle with a student (or his parents) over grades.

First, never argue with a student about his grade. Instead, when a student challenges the grades you have assigned, agree to review them on your own time. There is always the possibility you have miscalculated or made some mistake. If you have, you will be able to correct it without the added pressure of having your student looking over your shoulder. If, on the other hand, the grade is legitimate, you will be able to decide how to justify it to your student without having to think on the fly.

Second, never compare papers from one student to another. This is a trap into which you do not want to fall. During the school year, every teacher will have at least one student who claims he deserves more credit than he has been given. Invariably, his argument will rest on the fact that some other student in the class received more credit for work that was similar in nature to his own. If you agree to compare the papers, you have entered a battle you cannot win. If the work is even close to comparable, you will find yourself forced to either lower the grade of the student who scored higher, or to give added credit to a student you did not think deserved it. Your policy should be that any student may ask for a review of his grades, but that his work must stand on its own merit. His will be the only paper you review. Before reviewing, you should also let it be known that you will take away credit if you find any mistakes you missed the first time. If you actually enforce this policy, you will soon find that the only students challenging their grades are those who probably should.

Finally, make sure that every assignment you give contains at least one item that can be graded subjectively. This is your way of maintaining a healthy balance with your students. It provides you the opportunity to reward the hard working student and to challenge the lazy one. Ultimately, it gives you the ability to say that when it comes to educational decision making, you are the only one in the class who has the authority to do so.

Taking Attendance

Among the more ironic facts associated with the teaching profession is that, while teachers are hired to educate the students who attend their classes, one of their most important responsibilities involves keeping track of those who do not. No matter where you work as a teacher, attendance will be an issue. Dealing with it efficiently can save you a lot of time and headaches.

To do this, there is only one thing you should remember. Make your students as accountable for their absences as possible. The way in which you accomplish this will depend upon the age and relative maturity of your students. Young students must be given a great deal of direction in this regard, while high school students should be able to take full responsibility for making up any work they miss. In either case, the rule in your class should always be that a student returning from an absence should discuss his absence with you on the day he returns. Establish this as your policy and stick to it throughout the year. If you do, you will save yourself from a multitude of problems. By requiring your students to report to you upon their return, you guarantee yourself the opportunity to verify their reasons for absence, to make sure your attendance records are accurate, and to provide them with guidance regarding the work they missed and will need to complete. As a result, you will have a systematic approach to taking attendance that will minimize the energy required of you and ensure a minimum number of mistakes.

As a courtesy to your other students, make sure that anyone discussing absences with you does so at a time when it is appropriate. Just as you should take attendance during "down times" in the class period, make your students wait until there is a break in instruction before taking the time to discuss make up work. In this way, you will be sure that instructional time is not wasted by attendance taking procedures, and that a student who missed class time yesterday will not cause his classmates to miss class time today.

Completing Paperwork

Like it or not, teaching involves paperwork. The amount varies by district, but every school in the country does its part in keeping the nation's papermills humming. From impact forms to attendance records, education is a document intensive business. At times it can be overwhelming.

No teacher can successfully address the

entire volume of paperwork that is directed toward him in a single year. For a new teacher the problem can prove particularly vexing. Instinctively you know that all paperwork is not created equal, but you have no viable way to verify such a notion. Since you lack the experience enjoyed by veteran teachers, you are unaware of what separates the vital from the trivial. For you, every directive that comes your way has equal value attached. Handling any of it improperly would seem to lead to dire consequences. Yet you will not be able to handle it all. If you completed every piece of paperwork that crossed your desk, you would soon find yourself unable to address anything else. If you are not careful, paperwork will become like quicksand. It has been the downfall of many promising teachers.

You must find a way to address your paperwork while minimizing your energy loss. Basically there are three ways to do this. If you are the daring type who likes to live dangerously, you can simply ignore every request until it is made a second time. This way, you can immediately determine what is important by relying on the fact that unimportant matters will simply disappear. The main advantage to such an approach is that it clarifies the issue immediately. By the end of your first year, you will know exactly what paperwork you must do and what paperwork you can ignore. On the down side, this approach includes a high level of risk. Not only do you run the risk of forgetting a form that truly was vital, you also run the risk of gaining a reputation as someone who does not follow directions. Since this is not generally a good approach to take with your administration, this method is not highly recommended.

As an alternative, you can maintain a file of every directive sent your way during your first year of teaching. As you complete every form, graph, or table that comes to you, make a note of what response your efforts received. By year's end you will be able to distinguish between the truly important and the insignificant. While this will not help you during your first year of teaching, it will make you far more efficient during the rest of your career. You will be saving energy, but on a deferred plan.

If you would like to see an immediate minimizing of the time you spend on paperwork without appearing to be negligent, there is only one viable approach. Rely on the guidance of your mentors. For each item of paperwork you receive, ask them one simple question: How important is this? If they are talented, veteran teachers, they will have already figured it out. Follow their advice. Their collected wisdom could save you hours of valuable time.

Theory Into Practice

Only check your mailbox once per day. An empty mailbox is an open invitation for any administrator or secretary who is in search of a teacher who is "not too busy" to handle a miscellaneous task.

Attending Meetings

Teachers spend a great deal of time in meetings. Not all of it is time well spent. Unfortunately, meetings often provide teachers with their greatest source of frustration. A record of the meetings you attend during your career can easily become a chronicle of wasted time. How can you avoid this?

As a starting point, realize that not all meetings are as important to you as they are to the person who calls them. Often, you will find yourself receiving information at a meeting that you could just as easily have gleaned from a memo or a note in your maibox. When this happens there is little doubt that you will feel that your valuable time is being wasted.

To avoid this, a simple three step strategy can make your time spent in meetings far more productive. First, always find out what the purpose of the meeting is before you attend. By doing so, you are preparing yourself to be an insightful participant when the time for the meeting comes. This will allow you to ask articulate, well-informed questions, to add a positive influence to the group dynamic, and to help make the meeting more beneficial for your colleagues. Just as you will always enter your classroom prepared, you should enter every meeting prepared as well.

Second, set goals for yourself as a participant in the meeting. These can be simple but should always be significant. You may wish to have a question answered or may wish to share something that would benefit the group. Enter the meeting with a clear idea of what you would like to get out of it. If you then accomplish this goal, you will guarantee at least one reason to feel positive about the meeting.

Finally, do everything in your power to make the meeting short. Teachers are more willing than most professionals to work hard, but they become very sensitive when time begins to drag. While a well-timed question may make a meeting more profitable, too many questions will prolong it to the point where people get resentful. Be wary of expressing your opinion in a meeting, especially if you cannot state it succinctly. As a considerate colleague, discuss your most detailed questions and statements after the meeting has adjourned.

Inservice Training

Inservice training works for teachers as *A Tale of Two Cities* worked for Charles Dickens. It provides the best of times and the worst of times. On the one hand, you will receive some of the most useful information regarding your profession during inservice training. On the other hand, you will see some of the worst examples of teaching ever attempted. In the case of the high quality training, you need only apply the insights you have gained upon returning to the classroom. When faced with low quality inservice training, however, you must rely on a more sophisticated strategy.

In an ideal world, inservice training would never be considered grunt work. Unfortunately, that is exactly what it often becomes. Typically, the best inservice training is provided by classroom teachers who have taken it upon themselves to become involved in staff development. Unfortunately, most classroom teachers are not provided the time or the opportunity to conduct inservice training. In their place, you will encounter a wide variety of "educational consultants" who make their living by providing teachers with "insights" they would normally "never be exposed to in the classroom." The standard operating procedure among these "hired guns" is to reduce the entire process of education to a "workable model" which looks something like this:

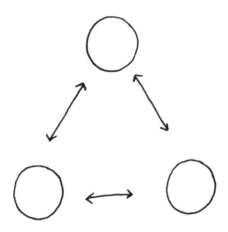

Having reduced education to a collection of circles and arrows, they will spend the first half of their presentation explaining why such an approach to teaching does not work. The second half of their presentation can then be devoted to "their model" of educational reform which will look something like this:

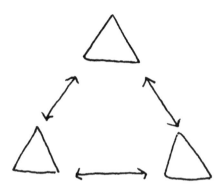

If you encounter such a presentation during your career, you can be sure of two things regarding the presenter:

1. He has not worked in the classroom for a very long time.

2. He was not very good when he did.

In such a situation, you must employ a very bold strategy if you are to avoid having your inservice training become a total waste of time. Just as with meetings, you should never enter an inservice session unprepared. In particular, you should have at least three or four very specific goals in mind for yourself as a workshop participant. If you find the session heading in an unproductive direction, politely but firmly explain your goals to the presenter. If you begin by saying, "Today I was hoping to learn . . . what can you tell me about it?" your instructor will be obligued to help you reach your goal. He, after all, is the expert. He is responsible for providing an answer. If, in the worst case, he is unable to do so, your colleagues will soon begin to dominate the meeting. Recognizing the presenter's inability to offer viable answers, they will begin to offer their own. As a result, you will gain the insight for which you are looking. This is inservice training as it should be: veteran teachers offering advice and insight to those in most need of receiving it. If the presenter of an inservice session is unable to offer anything useful to the workshop's participants, the participants should share insights among themselves.

There is one caveat. Not all educational consultants do a poor job. Many offer insights that you never could gain in the classroom. People like this deserve your utmost respect. If you encounter one, learn as much as you can. Yet when you encounter one of the many educational snake oil salesmen who frequent the inservice training circuit, it is your professional responsibility to challenge his credibility. If you do not, you will only perpetuate the paradigm that makes grunt work of a process that should improve the quality of education everywhere.

Final Thoughts

The good news about grunt work is that most school districts recognize it for what it is. To make life easier, a good school district will often provide guidelines to help its teachers complete their grunt work. Follow district guidelines. If, for example, there is a standard way for taking attendance in your district, follow it. It may not be the exact method you would have chosen on your own, but you save a great deal of time when you do not have to explain your own system. There are dozens of ways to be innovative and daring in the teaching profession. None of them involve grunt work. Just as there is no dynamic way to scrape a house, there is no flashy way to grade papers. When it comes to grunt work, it is best to just get it done.

If there are no guidelines available in your district, simply remember to minimize your energy loss. As you develop your own techniques and strategies, always ask yourself how you could do things more efficiently. Ultimately, your goal is to demonstrate excellence in the completion of your grunt work while at the same time preventing it from becoming a weight that drags you down. If you can accomplish these tasks without expending unreasonable amounts of energy, you will save your energy for more important things like teaching . . .

. . . plus any other tasks deemed necessary by the administration.

Chapter 10

The Best of Times
How to Know You Really Nailed It

If you talk to teachers who are honest, they will tell you that every so often they contemplate quitting their jobs. This usually happens when things are not going too well in their classrooms.

There is an ebb and flow associated with every school year. Some times are good and others are frustrating. No teacher has a perfect year, and no class is a perfect class. As the weather grows warmer and student attention spans grow shorter, it is easy to wonder sometimes if you are really accomplishing anything.

During my third year of teaching, this question became the topic of conversation for several teachers in my department. Each of us had endured several weeks in which little seemed to be happening in our classes. Faced with seemingly unmotivated and underachieving students, we were each nearing the end of our proverbial rope. At lunch, Pat wondered aloud whether any of us was having a positive effect on our students. Intrigued and concerned, we decided to ask them.

In the days that followed we developed a survey for our students. A two page questionnaire, it asked them to provide us with their honest opinions regarding life in our classrooms. What did they like best? What did they despise? Did they like us as teachers? Were we effective? In an effort to show our sincerity, we even asked our students if there was anything they wanted us to know but were afraid to say.

By Friday of the following week, our students had returned their surveys and we sat down to lunch and began to read each one out loud. I do not remember who first thought of the idea for the surveys but I do know why we all agreed to administer them. Deep down we all wanted some type of validation regarding our efforts as teachers. We all wanted an answer to Pat's question. As we read our students' comments, each of us received some measure of encouragement as we discovered what our students enjoyed about our classes. Still, we wondered if we were truly making a difference in the lives of our students. Was there really a good reason for us to stay in the profession?

Finally, as the lunch period neared its end, I was the only teacher still holding an unread survey. As all eyes in the room turned toward me, Pat smiled and said he hoped my last survey contained the insight for which we were all searching. Looking down at the paper, I realized that all of the questions had been left blank except one. In the space left for telling me his deepest thoughts, my student had placed his only answer. His statement was simple and to the point. "I think your all mising a cuppel of marbiles."

We all decided to keep teaching.

* * *

After all the preparing is done, your success as a teacher comes down to one thing: how well you teach. Likewise, how well you teach comes down to one thing: how well your students learn. When they learn well, there is no better feeling for a teacher. When they do not, there is nothing more frustrating.

This leaves you, as a new teacher, with some important questions to answer. How will you know that your students have truly learned? How will you be sure that you really did take advantage of all the teachable moments your students provided you? How will you know when you really nailed it? For each of these questions, you will only know the real answers if you look to your students. As was stated earlier, nothing is taught until something is learned. Therefore, if you want to know that you accomplished your goals as an educator, look to your students.

Yet how will you go about doing this? Test scores and class participation provide some level of knowledge. However, scores on evaluations can be misleading. Students who are active participants in class are not always those who have the best understanding. What you need is a qualitative yet objective way to know that your students are learning the lessons you are teaching. Fortunately, there is a way to accomplish this.

Ultimately, you will only know the degree to which your students have been impacted by your teaching when you observe their behavior. Test scores, homework grades and the like only tell you how well your students understand your evaluation system. Changed behavior tells you much more. Therefore, if you want to know the depth of understanding your students have, you must look at how they act.

This does not mean you are in search of personality changes as evidence for your successful teaching. Rather, it means there are specific behaviors which, when modeled, indicate a high level of understanding among your students. When you see these behaviors modeled by your students, you can be sure that they "get it."

Behaviors that Indicate Student Understanding

Behavior #1: Student reiteration

The first indicator that your students are learning well occurs when they begin to reiterate the ideas you have been attempting to teach. This can occur as a natural progression within the course of a lesson, or it might occur during a one-on-one conversation you are having with a student. When you hear your students begin to put the concepts you have been teaching into their own words, you will know they have crossed a threshold of understanding. You can be sure that your students are effectively processing the information at hand.

Often the reiteration process begins within the context of students asking questions. If a student prefaces his question with a qualifying statement such as, "Are you saying . . . ," this indicates that he has thought enough about the material to feel comfortable with trying to put it in his own terms. Paraphrasing, restating, and re-emphasizing are all higher order thinking processes that require a depth of analysis on the part of the student. Before he can attempt any of these, a student must make the concept in question his own intellectual property. To do so requires both attention to detail and clarity of purpose. The student who is able to accomplish this has most assuredly added the ideas in question to the long list of things he has learned during his lifetime.

It is therefore vital for a teacher to encourage reiteration if she wishes to be an effective educator. She must also use her students' reiteration of ideas as a stepping stone toward deeper learning. This can be accomplished in a variety of ways, each of which depends upon the accuracy of the student's original attempt at verbalizing the ideas. Basically there are three possibilities: A student can be totally accurate in his analysis, partially correct, or just flat wrong. Each scenario warrants a different response but also presents a unique opportunity.

When a student is wrong in his analysis of a concept, it is a mistake to think that this is a bad thing. The important fact in such a case is that he made an attempt to process the information you were trying to teach. A student who tries to verbalize his understanding and does so incorrectly is still better off than a student who sits in silence and never makes the attempt. Your response in such a circumstance can make the difference between whether your student becomes enlightened or simply more confused. Two things are absolutely essential. First, you must tell the student he is wrong. This may sound like a simple thing to do but it is far from easy. Because many students are convinced that "right" answers are their ultimate goal, you run the risk of discouraging them when you tell them their facts are not accurate. Even so, you must be sure to correct misinformation. It is even more important that you get your student to focus on the fact that quality thinking is more significant than correct answers, so the second thing you must do when confronted with an incorrect response is to make sure you point out the areas in which your student thought well. By doing this, you will empower him to be more bold in proposing answers in the future. Rather than shying away from questions, he will become convinced that, while his facts may have been confused, his thought process was appropriate. He will continue thinking. With any luck, this will lead him to more accurate responses as well.

When a student offers a response that is partially correct, you have a situation that offers you many opportunities to teach. "Half right" answers provide you with some of the most significant teachable moments you will encounter. A "half right" answer indicates, to one degree or another, that your student has already gained some insight from your teaching. By the time he can even offer a partially valid response, the light bulb in his mind has already turned bright. Yet there is still room to improve the thinking process as well as make sure that the incorrect notions are set straight. Your job in this case is two-fold. See the gaps. Then fill them. If your student was able to offer a partially valid response it means that he was at least on the right track toward understanding. Something kept his understanding from being complete. You must find out not only what he was thinking, but how he was thinking. How did he arrive at his conclusion? By asking questions regarding his thought process, you will be able to see where it was inadequate. Chances are he will see it too. When he does, he will have learned far more than how to provide a correct answer.

Finally, if a student accurately verbalizes the ideas you have been teaching, you are in the best possible teaching situation. By effectively paraphrasing the original idea, your student has taken the first step in transforming the information you presented into something useful that he will never forget. This is only the first step along the road toward full understanding. If you leave the student here, you have only given him a new piece of trivia to add to his mind's file drawer. To make his learning experience more complete, you must lead him immediately toward recognizing the implications of what he has learned. This means you must give him additional ideas to ponder. If he correctly describes the concept you are teaching, praise him for the accuracy of his response. Immediately ask him how his newfound understanding would apply in a real life or hypothetical scenario. This forces him to move to the next level of understanding which involves . . .

Behavior #2: Student synthesis

The second step on the road to full understanding occurs when your students begin to synthesize new ideas and insights using the material they have learned in your class. Synthesis occurs when your students use the material you have presented to develop new and original ideas of their own. This can occur naturally, but it can also be encouraged.

To understand how this process can be encouraged, you must look at the nature of the process itself. Before students will build something with their ideas, they must be provided a reason to do so. A teacher can force the issue by imposing a reason. The simplest way to accomplish this is to provide students with an appropriate assignment. If you use this method, you should seek to provide assignments which prompt your students to synthesize using the material you have covered in class.

As an example, consider a math teacher who wishes to teach her students the difference between two-dimensional and three-dimensional objects. In a typical classroom, this lesson would be taught by providing numerous examples of each type of object. The teacher could show her students two-dimensional objects such as leaves, signs, and sheets of paper. For three-dimensional objects, she could show them acorns, pine cones, and flashlights. In order to lead her students through the process of reiterating what they have been taught, she need only have them provide her with additional examples. To take her students to the point of synthesis, however, she must lead them to a higher level of thinking. Rather than providing examples of two-dimensional and three-dimensional objects, she could have her students build three-dimensional models from two-dimensional blueprints. To do this, her students must have a complete understanding of both two-dimensional and three-dimensional objects. In addition, they must recognize how one is related to the other and how to mentally "travel" from one dimension to the next. Had they been asked only to provide examples of each type of object, the students would have learned the facts in isolation. They would likely see little or no connection between the concepts. By providing an appropriate assignment that forces them to synthesize, she also encourages them to attain a much greater depth of understanding. If she is a truly excellent teacher, she will lead them to even greater owner-ship of knowledge by allowing them to practice the behavior which will make their understanding most complete. . .

Behavior #3: Student teaching

The wisdom to associate with this behavior is the age old adage that "to teach is to learn twice." You will enter the classroom during your first year with a profound knowledge of your subject matter. When you return to school the following year, you will possess an even deeper understanding. Why? You will understand more of your subject matter simply because you have taught it for a year. This process will continue. Each year that you return to the classroom, you will be more confident about your understanding of your subject. Consequently, you will be more confident in your proficiency as a teacher.

To teach well, you must not only think of the subject you are teaching, but of the students who are learning. Not only must you think of how to understand the material itself, but you must also think of how to present it in such a way that your students will understand it. Significantly, thinking about how to teach a subject is among the best ways to learn it. While learning a subject, teachers automatically go through the first two steps of reiterating and synthesizing the information they learn. This allows them to become highly knowledgeable regarding the subject at hand. When considering how to present the material, however, teachers take their learning to an entirely new level.

It should be obvious that students can benefit by engaging in the same process. Students who teach other students learn much more than students who do not. Therefore, you should allow your students to teach one another as often as they can. There are many ways to accomplish this. One of the simplest ways to provide your students with this opportunity is to allow them to help one another with homework and other assignments. If students are working on assignments in class, allow them to work together with a partner. If you wish students to first attempt these assignments on their own, then let those who finish quickly (and accurately!) assist those who work more slowly. Students will think they are simply discussing the work with their peers. In reality, they are processing, reiterating, synthesizing, and presenting the information at hand. There can be no better way for them to demonstrate their understanding. As a teacher, you will know you have done your best when your students begin to do your job.

The best classrooms are those which provide students the opportunity to demonstrate the behaviors described above. Keep this in mind as you plan for success in your classroom. Build into your teaching methodology opportunities for your students to reiterate, to synthesize, and to teach. Force the issue if you must.

Your greatest success will come on those days when your students display these behaviors without being forced. It will begin innocently enough, with one of your students trying in vain to accurately describe a concept in his own words. Before you can offer words of correction, another student will offer them for you and the class debate will have begun. On their own initiative, your students will discuss the finer points of what you have been trying to teach them, clarifying, arguing, providing point and counterpoint. Soon one student who has somehow gained more wisdom than the others will make the one statement that ties everything together and provides clarity to everyone's understanding. He will ask you if he got it right and you will tell him that he did. You will be proud of your students and they will be proud of themselves. The bell will ring, signaling the end of the day, and the hallways will soon grow quiet. You will sit smiling in your silent classroom, confident that you still have your marbiles after all.

Theory Into Practice

Among the most difficult things you will need to learn as a beginning teacher is how to observe your students. Avoid the temptation of paying too much attention to your own efforts. Since there are so many tasks for which you are responsible, it is easy to get caught up in the trap of worrying about what you need to do. In order to know if your students are learning, you must focus on your students rather than yourself. Consider employing the following strategies:

- Talk with your students outside of class.
Find out what they understand and what they do not. These "interviews" allow you to gain insight from your students while neither of you is under pressure to perform.

- Watch your students while they work in class. Don't grade papers or take attendance. Just sit and watch. Make mental notes regarding your impressions. You will quickly realize who is struggling, who is comfortable, and who is motivated.

- Ask your students how you are doing.
By gaining their honest appraisal of your teaching abilities, you will learn how they perceive your class. This will allow you to effectively troubleshoot when problems arise.

Chapter 11

The Worst of Times
When It Isn't Your Fault
(but feels like it is)

If you teach long enough, you will eventually come face to face with tragedy. Of the tragedies you will face, none is worse than the death of a student. I encountered this harsh reality one weekend during my second year of teaching.

As weekends go, it began with great promise. Friday dawned bright and clear with temperatures warm enough to make the winter season short, even by Florida standards. As the early morning bell rang to signal the start of the week's last day of school, classes were a formality. The weekend had already begun.

Among the students there was an air of excitement that went beyond the usual end-of-the-week enthusiasm. Spring break was only two weeks away, and for the seniors, trips to Daytona Beach were in the final stages of planning. As a prelude, students had organized a beach volleyball tournament for Saturday afternoon. In this week between the winter and spring sports seasons, even the athletes would get the chance to play just for the fun of it. Several parties were planned for Saturday night.

Throughout the day, conversations ranged from weekend plans to college acceptances. Most students had received their acceptance letters in the previous weeks; many talked freely about their hopes and dreams, knowing now that they could afford to have some. Few conversations focused on subject matter. Little was taught regarding biology, English, or math. Nobody seemed to mind.

By mid-afternoon, all semblance of institutional control seemed to have disappeared. Much as it happens on the final day of school or the day before a major vacation, teachers and administrators attempted at first to reign in their students, then recognized they were fighting a losing battle, and finally just sat down to visit with their kids. Dozens of teachers found reasons for moving their classes outside. The day ended without incident, mainly because no one was looking for one. Late in the afternoon, thunderstorms rolled through the entire county.

At daybreak on Saturday morning, a warm sun broke through a lone cloud on the horizon. For the rest of the daylight hours, the day was one of postcard perfection. The volleyball tournament hastily arranged by a small group of students quickly evolved into a barbeque and then an evening bonfire. Most of the senior class participated at one point or another. The thunderstorms so typical of Florida afternoon weather held off until just after dark. With the bonfire dampened, most students finalized plans regarding the rest of the night. Slowly at first, then in increasing numbers, cars pulled one by one away from the beach and headed back toward town. Turning left along the North-South coast highway, they crossed the causeway near Dragon Point and entered town ten minutes later. Only one car turned to the right.

Taking the coast highway north along the beach involved a trip that was far from the beaten path. Running parallel to the waves breaking relentlessly on the shore, the rail-straight high-way soon left streetlights and other signs of civilization behind. To the right, wind-swept sand dunes were held in their place by wild sea oats. To the left, palm trees and wax myrtle swayed their dark silhouettes in the breeze of the moonless night. Ahead lay the seldom-used causeway which offered the next link to the mainland. Twenty minutes after leaving the beach, the car and its three occupants crossed the causeway and returned to the solid surface of the mainland. Turning onto a dark and winding road, they began the slow journey back to town from the north.

No one outside the car will ever know why its occupants chose this route home. The two young men who died in the eventual accident can offer no explanation. The driver, the only survivor, has chosen not to tell. In the days that followed, there were hundreds of speculations offered. None seemed in any way appropriate. All that was known was the horrible result. Traveling along the rain-slicked road at a high rate of speed, the car failed to negotiate a sharp left turn. Skidding along the road's surface, it crossed the shoulder and slid down the roadside embankment to the edge of the canal below. There it rolled gently onto its passenger side, then eventually to its roof as the car's weight slowly forced it into the mud. Pinned inside, the driver listened in horror as his friends first screamed for help, then gasped for breath, then grew silent beneath the water that was slowly filling the car. With his own head only inches from the rising water, the driver and his car finally came to rest. In the daylight of the next morning, the wreckage was spotted by a passing motorist. Alcohol was determined to be a contributing factor in the accident.

On Monday morning, the joy of the previous Friday had been completely forgotten. Where there had so recently been such freedom and laughter, there was now only the sound of quiet sobbing. In their classes, the members of the senior class did their best to cope. Stricken by the loss of two classmates, they feared also for a third who lay in an area hospital in critical condition. It would be three weeks before they knew that he was finally in the clear. By Wednesday, teachers throughout the school did their best to return things to normal. It was a painful but necessary process. By Thursday, students began making eye contact again.

Once more, Friday dawned clear and warm. This time, however, the frivolity of the previous week was replaced with a tangible silence. When students did speak, they spoke only of how guilty they felt. No parties were planned for the weekend.

In the months that followed, the driver of the car continued the long and tortuous healing process necessitated by his injuries. The rest of the students struggled to recover from their own loss as well. To hear them talk at first, I wondered if they would ever be young again. Slowly though, the smiles returned to their faces, the laughter to their hearts. Dozens received counseling to help them through their grief.

By mid April, the driver began to receive homebound instruction from teachers sent to his hospital room. Continuing his physical therapy and renewing his studies, he hoped to be graduated with his classmates in June. The teaching staff was hopeful this would provide closure.

When June came, however, closure was never found. For the students whose friends had died in the accident, seeing the driver receive his diploma was like reopening the deepest of wounds. Rather than provide closure, the driver's return inspired resentment and anger. Although many of them had been drinking on that fateful night, they felt anger that the driver had chosen to drive. When reminded that they had made the same choice, they grew angry that he had crashed. As graduation day approached, the level of tension grew steadily.

With apprehension I took my seat near the back of the auditorium at graduation. To his credit, my principal quickly made the ceremony as positive as it rightly should have been. No mention was made of the accident, but a respectful moment of reflection was honored as a way of giving thanks for the students who had made it to this day. No explanation was necessary. Excitement built as we worked our way through the obligatory speeches, the invocation, and the National Anthem. Flashbulbs popped. Balloons slipped from the hands of younger brothers and sisters and floated toward the ceiling. Throughout the audience, waves of recognition and shouts of joy traveled between graduates and their family members. One by one, the Class of 1988 walked across the stage to receive diplomas.

Then the name of the driver was called.

Slowly he rose from his seat and started the longest journey of his young life. Unlike the graduates who had gone before him or those who would come later, he received no polite applause from the crowd or cheers from his family. For the first time that day, the auditorium grew silent but for the sound of halting steps across the wood floor of the stage. In the audience, three mothers wept quietly. Shakily, the driver reached for the principal's hand and received his diploma. Then life went on.

Near the back of the auditorium, I mourned the loss of three lives.

Chapter 12

Saving Yourself
Preserving Your Sanity While You Teach

In an effort to show her students the importance of prayer, a Sunday School teacher once offered the following lesson. Taking a bag of whole walnuts, a large jar, and a five pound bag of rice, she placed the items before her class. Removing the lid from the jar, she first poured the entire five pounds of rice into the open vessel. When she was done, about two inches of empty space remained beneath the jar's lip. Opening the bag of walnuts, she proceeded to place as many of them as would fit in the space that remained. With some struggle, she was able to fit half the bag, six walnuts, between the top of the rice and the lid which she then screwed tightly onto the jar. Her students were unimpressed.

Moving a large bowl from a nearby table,

the teacher proceeded to empty the contents of the jar into it. Placing the empty jar back on the table in front of her, she then placed each of her walnuts, twelve walnuts in all, into the jar. Pausing for effect, she then went on to fill the jar with five pounds of rice. Because the walnuts had gone in first, the rice was able to squeeze into all the small spaces that were left between the shells. The entire five pounds of rice was able to fit in the jar with room to spare!

The lesson for her class? Do the important things first and you will still have room for everything else.

* * *

One day you will look back on your career instead of forward. In the years between, you will leave your mark on the lives and futures of thousands of students. If you are fortunate, someone will consider you worth remembering.

It is only in looking back on your time in the classroom that you will gain a small measure of understanding regarding the significance of your impact as a teacher. Through your efforts as a teacher, you will have influenced both your students and your profession. Your school community will be changed simply because of your presence. Although you will never know the full measure of your influence, you can be sure that your teaching will change the lives of your students in ways beyond your imagination. What you may not realize is how much teaching will change you.

Teaching, by its very nature, is a profession that can be all-consuming. There is literally no end to the amount of compassion and empathy you will need to display, or the number of jobs you will have to do. For many educators, teaching becomes the sole focus of life. As a new teacher, you must find a way to prevent this from happening.

At first this may sound like a counter-intuitive statement. It is nonetheless true. While it is important for you to become adept and fluid in your teaching style, you cannot afford to have teaching become the only thing you do. If it does, you will soon find yourself consumed by the very profession to which you have dedicated your life. Nothing will shorten your career faster. You must live the life of a teacher without being consumed by it.

As a beginning teacher, you are your great-est asset. Fresh from college, industry, or some other walk of life, your perspectives will prove new and exciting to your students. They will quickly recognize the value of your life experience precisely because it extends beyond what you do as a teacher. Likewise, they will respect your views on the world beyond education because they will see that you were able to succeed in it. Because you are able to show them a side of yourself that extends beyond your teaching, they will admire the multi-dimensional nature of your character.

Yet before long, you will find your teaching responsibilities influencing every aspect of your life. Weekends will consist of lesson planning and paper grading. Evenings during the week will be spent on parent phone calls and a host of after school activities. Taking note of your dedication, your principal may ask for your help on a number of committees. Soon you will have little time for yourself. What little time you do have, you will spend pursuing the one thing you now need most: sleep.

You cannot afford to live this way. Not only will it drag you down as an individual, it will make you an ineffective teacher. Sadly, this is the life experience of most first year teachers. Wanting to do the best job possible, they become convinced that they must focus strictly on their jobs. Yet, nothing could be farther from the truth. The sad fact is that every waking hour could be devoted to teaching and there would still be more work to do. You will never get it all done. If you try, you will soon find yourself struggling to maintain forward momentum as an educator. Consumed by the sheer volume of responsibility that is now yours, you will find your energy level steadily dropping as you try to solve everyone's problems while consistently neglecting your own. In the end, you will burn out. Before sharing yourself with others, make sure you have something left to give.

What follows are ten practical suggestions for protecting your professional sanity. To put them in the proper context, consider them as ways to save yourself from teacher burnout. The list is by no means exhaustive, nor is it sequenced in order of importance.

10 Ways for Teachers to Maintain Their Professional Mental Health

#1: Maintain friendships with non-teachers.

Unless you attend a college which trains only teachers, your college years introduce you to people with a wide variety of interests. Part of what makes the college experience complete is the opportunity to rub shoulders with people who wish to be engineers, accountants, lawyers, and journalists. In the college environment, this wide variety of interests provides for a dynamic interplay of people and personalities. It is what makes college fun.

Upon entering the classroom, you will find yourself standing before students with an equally wide range of personalities and interests. Like your friends in college, some of your students will grow up to be engineers, accountants, lawyers and journalists as well. In the classroom setting, this wide range of future hopes will make your class that much more fun to teach. The variety of interests and personalities you find among your students will keep you constantly alert, excited and intrigued.

In your personal life, you must maintain a similar dynamic. While you will have many friends who are teachers, you must also have some that are not. If everyone you know is a teacher, you will only gain a teacher's view on everything. Life will quickly become too introspective and stilted. To maintain your objectivity regarding how the world operates, and to remain alert, excited and intrigued about the world around you, maintain friendships with people who have no connections with education. Not only will they provide stories for you to tell your students, they will keep your intellect challenged, your emotions balanced, and your perspective clear. At times the only one who can analyze a situation accurately is someone who is uninvolved. For this reason alone, it is worth your time to maintain friendships with non-teaching friends.

#2: Protect family time.

Even if you are a family of one, it is important to protect family time. If you are part of a family of more than one, it is even more important. Teaching is time-consuming and it is too easy to neglect the ones you love. Therefore, be sure to protect and preserve time for your family during the school year. If you are a parent or a spouse, it is not enough to promise your mate and your kids that you will have more free time in the summer. Marriage and parenting are year-round jobs. On average, the divorce rate among teachers is slightly lower than in other segments of the population. Yet a consistent difficulty within teachers' families involves the negative effects of school-related problems on the home. More often than not, this takes the form of time being stolen from the family in order to solve school-related problems. Avoid the ironic situation of having your efforts to help someone else's family become a source of struggle within your own.

#3: Make the most of summer vacation.

June, July and August provide teachers with some unique opportunities not available in any other profession. Like most professionals, you will work the number of hours associated with a twelve month work year. Unlike most professionals, these hours will be compressed into a ten month period. As a result, late June through late August provide you with hours of "profession free" time. While you may need to work in order to make ends meet, you will not have to teach. This will leave you with many hours to pursue other interests.

If you can, travel during your summer vacation. In particular, go someplace with which you are unfamiliar. There are few things that will renew your sense of well-being faster than participating in an adventure. Sometimes travel to a new locale is just what you need. If you are unable to travel away from home, consider exploring the unusual places in your own neighborhood. Day trips and weekends away do wonders for the soul. If you can afford it, take the summer off. If you must work, consider trying to . . .

#4:   Work a new job each summer.

Your main source of income will keep you occupied for ten months of the year. If this is not enough to pay the bills, you will find yourself in need of temporary employment during the summer. Since this employment is temporary, why not try your hand at a wide variety of occupations? Not only will you cover your financial obligations, but you will gain tremendous insight into the wide variety of marketable skills employed in the workplace. This will help you as a teacher when you share your experience with your students. Showing them that you have been able to achieve success in a number of diverse settings will increase their respect for you. In addition, you will gain the added benefit of knowing what employers are looking for in the workplace. This is valuable information you can share with your students as they prepare for life after schooling.

On a more personal level, trying your hand at a number of different jobs can be a lot of fun. One teacher, during a five year period, spent his summers reviewing books, painting houses, testing children's toys, writing curriculum, and working with NASA. Only the curriculum writing assignment was directly related to his full-time job. Even so, his experience with the other jobs provided numerous rich experiences which he could later translate into effective lessons for his students. While providing for his financial well-being, he was also making his classroom a more interesting place for his students.

If nothing else, working a variety of summer jobs during your teaching career will keep you from getting bored or predictable. Also, it will provide you with countless anecdotes with which to entertain your teaching colleagues. After a few years, you will have gained the reputation of someone who does daring and unusual things with his summers. Your colleagues will look forward to hearing your tales when September rolls around.

#5: Pursue a dream.

Whether during the summer or during the school year, always pursue your dreams. Of the many things you can do as a teacher to preserve your sanity, this may be the most important. It is a real danger for any teacher, especially a new one, that he may become so devoted to the task of teaching that other key aspects of his life might get squeezed out of existence. If this happens to you, you may find yourself losing an important part of your personal identity. Before long, you will find yourself with little to offer anyone.

To avoid this, make a conscious effort to make your personal dreams a priority. Pay attention to your life-long goals and ambitions. Learn to play the saxophone like you always wanted. Write a novel. Climb Mount Everest! Whatever dream you choose to pursue, make it enough of a priority that you can achieve steady and consistent progress toward it. If you need to, write out a long-term plan. Simply make sure that you remain a dreamer throughout your years as a teacher. If you do not, you will have no way of convincing your students to dream either.

Theory Into Practice

To make sure that teaching does not become the focus of your entire life, complete the following exercise:

Write a list of 100 things you would like to do during your life-time. Once your list is complete, get to work. One by one, do the things about which you have always dreamed. Accomplishing your goals will be among the most encouraging things you will ever experience. What happens when you complete all 100?

Write a new list!

#6: Get involved with kids of different ages.

Teachers love working with kids but often do not recognize when they are getting too much of a good thing. Go to most church youth groups, boys' and girls' clubs, or Little Leagues, and you will not have to look very far before you see your first teacher. Countless teachers spend all day working with their students, only to spend their nights and weekends volunteering to work with kids somewhere else. They do this because they love kids.

Yet there is a danger inherent in this practice. Before long, a teacher runs a real risk of feeling that his entire life revolves around children. This is not necessarily a bad thing, but can certainly lead to a feeling of being trapped. If things are not going well at school, sometimes the best strategy is to get away from it all for a while. If, however, a teacher leaves a bad day at the office only to go to a frustrating time at the Little League field, feelings of resentment are inevitable.

One simple rule can help you avoid this. If you desire to work with children beyond your hours at school, just make sure they are not the same age as the children you teach. If you teach fourth graders, work with your church's teenage youth group. If you teach high school, coach Little League. By taking this approach, you will guarantee that the problems you face in school will not be repeated while you are doing your volunteer work. You will face problems, but they will be different problems. Sometimes this can actually be refreshing.   After a day of struggling through Shakespeare with high school seniors, teaching an eight year old how to play basketball might provide just the relief you need.

#7: Avoid teaching year-round.

Each school year, every teacher in America is given the opportunity to teach summer school. If you agree to do this, you not only will push yourself to the point of exhaustion before the regular school year starts, you will also gain little benefit from the experience. Summer school is so far removed from the normal classroom experience that it offers little insight to a person who wishes to learn how to become a better teacher. Summer school is best taught by those teachers who are confident in their own abilities and have many years of experience under their belts. Neither of these attributes applies to you as a new teacher. You would be better off staying home.

#8: Talk teaching, not education.

When people find out you are a teacher, they will want to talk. As a teacher, you will soon find out that no one is neutral regarding educational issues. Everybody has an opinion regarding how education should be done.

For the most part, people you meet during the course of your career will be very positive regarding what you do. Some, however, will have an axe to grind. Involving yourself in a lengthy conversation with such a person will prove both frustrating and depressing. To avoid this situation, adhere to this simple rule: talk teaching, not education.

Conversations about education degrade too easily. Conversations about teaching remain far more positive. If given the chance, almost everyone can recount a horror story from their years in school. Somewhere, somehow, they were wronged by teachers who remain, in their eyes, mean-spirited, harsh and inept. Just as easily, people can be lead into debates regarding the effectiveness of local schools, the outrageousness of school taxes, or a host of other controversial topics about education. Yet, when coaxed a little bit, people can also recount charming stories of how special teachers helped make them who they are today. Make sure you lead conversations in this direction. Ask people to tell you about their favorite teachers. Have them recount their favorite school memories. At the end of your time together, you will both be far more encouraged than you would have been had you discussed school board policy or the annual budget.

#9: Volunteer.

If you are the altruistic type (as most teachers are) consider devoting some of your time to volunteer work. There is no limit to the number of opportunities available to someone, with the qualifications and skills of a teacher, who wants to volunteer. Because teachers are required to do a number of different jobs within their typical work days, they are exactly the type of flexible people most volunteer agencies are seeking. As a result, volunteering can afford you an opportunity to feel good about serving your community that extends far beyond the services you offer in the classroom.

If your desire is not only to offer your services but also to find a way to relieve tension, consider volunteering in a situation where no one knows you are a teacher. You will still be able to use your problem solving skills to your greatest advantage, but will not be the center of attention as you are in the classroom. Volunteering will provide a release from stress rather than an added burden. If you really desire to put teaching out of your mind for a while, do volunteer work that is unlike anything you do in your classroom. Build houses for Habitat for Humanity. Walk for the March of Dimes. Whatever activity you choose, you will feel satisfied and encouraged because you have helped someone in need.

#10: Maintain a support group.

The first nine suggestions listed in this chapter provide ways to reduce or eliminate the stress that inevitably comes with teaching. Eventually, teaching will cause you frustration. Where it comes from is unimportant. What matters is that you get help. When you find yourself stressed by the pressures of being a devoted teacher, it is vital that you have someone who can help you through the rough times. Therefore, establishing and maintaining a support system is among the most important things you must do as a beginning teacher.

Your support group need not be formal in its structure or function. It can be as simple as having two or three colleagues with whom to discuss your frustrations. What matters is that you have a place to turn when things get difficult. Early in the school year, make a mental note of which colleagues you would seek out if you had a problem. Seek their advice when you encounter your first unreasonable parent. Ask for their help in reaching a difficult student. If nothing else, a group of colleagues who offer support will continually remind you that you are not alone in this process.

Beyond seeking their advice, make sure you get involved socially with the colleagues who comprise your support network. Never underestimate the therapeutic value of getting together with friends and laughing away your troubles. You will be amazed at how much better you feel about teaching if you and your colleagues go out for pizza after a tough day. One caveat with which to end this section: Never let your support group become a collection of whiners. It is true that teaching can be a difficult and demanding job. It is also true that no job is more rewarding. Surround yourself with people who focus on the rewards rather than the problems.

A Lesson in Saving Yourself

Like the Sunday School students mentioned earlier, you will need to establish your priorities if you wish to be successful. Your "walnuts" will need to be the first thing you place in the jar. This simple lesson regarding the priority of prayer is no less applicable for you with regard to teaching. If you spend your time addressing the seemingly "urgent" things, you may not have room for the truly important ones.

As you work through your career, never lose sight of the fact that you need to take care of yourself as an individual. To be an effective teacher requires a delicate balance between being selfish and being selfless. If you are selfish enough to think only of yourself, you will find yourself alone as an educator, rejected by your students, and ignored by your peers. On the other hand, if you are selfless to the point of ignoring your own needs as a human being, you will find yourself exhausted by the amount of emotional energy you have expended. Without an appropriate balance, you will have nothing to offer the students you want so much to help. Before you save the world, make sure you take good care of yourself.

Chapter 13

Farewell
What It Means to Be a Teacher

Legend has it that a wise teacher once decided to teach his students about the value of having vision. Holding an acorn aloft, he asked them what they saw. After a few puzzled looks came their incredulous reply.

"That's an acorn!"

"I'm afraid you lack vision," he responded. "You only see what is, not what might be."

Feeling enlightened, his best student smiled and raised her hand in order to venture another guess.

"What do you see now?" the teacher asked.

"I get it now," said the girl, "I see a tree."

Lowering the acorn, the teacher looked intently into the eyes of his students. "Do you all see a tree?"

Around the room heads nodded in affirmation.

"I'm afraid you still lack vision," said the teacher, "for I see a forest."

What ever became of Rita Steiner? Are she and Jennifer Jones still the best of friends? Every day for an entire year, they entered my class inseparable. Like a right hand that fits perfectly within a left, so was the nature of their relationship. Never have I taught two students who complemented one another more effectively. In my home I still have a picture taken with them at their graduation. Smiling, I am standing between them with my arms over each of their shoulders. This is entirely appropriate. A picture with only one of them would seem incomplete.

Somewhere Jerry Schultz, the favorite student of my first year of teaching, is living a life I was able to influence. No longer the boy of eighteen I once knew, he is a man of thirty-three. Where he is, or what he has made of his life, I may never know, but for as long as I live I will wonder. Was he able to reach the unlimited potential that I could see in him so clearly, but which he himself was seemingly never able to grasp?

In the same way, I wonder about other students I have had the privilege of teaching. Has Nicole Purka remained the compassionate person I once knew? What ever happened to Jeff Parker or Emily Calcagno? Is Laura Greiner happy after all these years? These are the thoughts that remain in the heart of a teacher. Wherever my students are, I continue to wonder. Have their lives been enriched as a result of their time in my class?

I often wonder what forests now grow as a result of my work as a teacher. What fruit has grown from the seeds I have sown in the hearts and minds of my former students? Although I may never know the answers to these questions, I will continue to wonder. I will wonder because I have learned to see the potential of each student. I have learned that in every child there is some form of genius and some driving passion. Most of all, I have learned to see a forest in every acorn.

What do I see when I look back on fifteen years spent in front of the classroom? What wisdom have I gained? Perhaps the story of the acorn represents it best. In this simple tale of a man and an acorn lies all the truth you need to become an excellent teacher.

Many years ago, I was a first year teacher working in Florida. Newly married and having just purchased a home, I was befriended by a guest who was visiting my neighbor. In town for the winter months, he was one of what Floridians sarcastically refer to as "snowbirds." Each afternoon he would return from his daily fishing trip, and I would return from work. During one of our many conversations across the backyard fence, I discovered that he was a recently retired teacher. I had been in the classroom for less than five months. He had just left his classroom after thirty-five years.

As the weeks passed, I looked more and more forward to our afternoon discussions. It was a true delight to share the day's experience with someone who had "been there." For three months, I enjoyed my chats with Les in the backyard. From him I learned many of my most valuable lessons as a rookie teacher. In February he left to return north.

In the months that followed, Les and I occasionally corresponded through the mail. I think I even called him once. With each of us leading busy lives, it was difficult to maintain contact, but we did our best. Every now and then I found myself employing some of his sage advise in the classroom and whispering a quiet "Thanks Les" under my breath. By the time spring rolled around, however, I found myself thinking of him less and less. By September and the start of the new school year, he was a distant memory.

Maybe that's why it was such a surprise to feel a rush of joy when Les pulled into my neighbor's driveway the following December. Without a second thought, I was out to the back fence yelling his name as he stepped from the car. We were deep in conversation long before his host ever knew he had arrived. We picked up right where we had left off, as if he had never left. For the next three months, I learned the lessons of a second year teacher, all across the backyard fence. The following year my training continued.

Then my neighbor sold his house.

I wonder about Les a lot these days. I have thought of him often as I have penned these pages. Looking back, I realize the profound influence that he, and others, have had on my career as an educator. Knowing what I now know, I am sure that he was an excellent teacher.

Yet how do I know? I know because I saw in Les the qualities that the last fifteen years have taught me are characteristic of excellent teachers. No longer standing before twenty-five high school sophomores, Les still recognized a student when he saw one. In me he could have seen an acorn. Instead he saw a forest. That is what excellent teachers do.

The road toward excellence in teaching extends before you. As a beginning teacher, you must learn the qualities of empathy, compassion and dedication that provide for excellence in teaching. More importantly, you must learn to employ them in your own life and career. As you begin your journey, be ever mindful that your actions will speak far louder than your words; your compassion will accomplish far more than your intellect. You can only teach what you are willing to live.

Through it all, your vision of what teaching should be will shape your destiny. Much like the man who saw a forest in the simplest seed, you will need to see what is sometimes only visible in the imagination. Although teaching can be filled with joy, it can also be tedious and frustrating. It is a marathon, not a sprint. In the times when you wonder how you will continue, only a strong sense of vision will keep you going. For this reason alone, it is worth the effort to maintain a positive vision regarding your profession. At times this will require hours of thought, introspection, and work. It is still worth the effort. When you can only see acorns, it is time to rethink what you are doing.

As you develop a vision for who you wish to be as a teacher, think back to those teachers who influenced you. Choose excellent teachers after whom to model yourself and then diligently work to emulate them as you teach. If imitation is the greatest form of flattery, you could pay no greater tribute to a former teacher than to model your career after his. More importantly, you will be maintaining a tradition that has long existed in the teaching profession. Excellent teachers inspire their best students to become excellent teachers for the next generation. It has always been so and it always will be. For the excellent teacher this a guarantee of immortality.

In the end, however, you will not become an excellent teacher because you were able to maintain a healthy vision of your profession throughout your career. You will not become an excellent teacher by simply modeling your career after an example of excellence who came before you. Ultimately, you will only become an excellent teacher if you work diligently, every day, to change the world. This, in the final analysis, is what teaching is all about.

As a teacher, you are a participant in the greatest of professions. From your profession all other paths of life find their common root. As a teacher, you are a molder of futures, a shaper of dreams. From you students will gain a sense of importance, of hope, and of destiny. They will enter your classroom in September and they will leave, changed, in June. You will leave an indelible mark on their lives whether you or they realize it. Yours is the power to make their lives better or worse.

With this in mind, you will only succeed as a teacher if you realize that each day you are changing the world. If your purpose, through the diligent application of your skill, is to change it for the better, you have all the requisite qualifications for being an excellent teacher. You need only to go out and do it. Yet, as a beginning teacher, you may find this intimidating. What ability do you have to change the world for the better? How would you even go about it? Beyond that, do you have the right to take on such a responsibility?

As an educator, you do have the right to change the world. In fact, it is expected of you. It is an inherent responsibility associated with your chosen profession. As for how you do it, this is more a function of providing your students an example than anything else. By working diligently at your profession, you will teach them a proper work ethic. By being compassionate, you will teach them compassion. By standing up for what you believe, you will teach them integrity. By admitting your mistakes, you will show them the value of being an honest human being. In the meantime, you will have the privilege of sharing with them the love you have for the subject you teach. What more noble profession could you have chosen? As an excellent teacher you will change the world. How will you do it? One student at a time.

Index

T

U

W

If you would like to order additional copies of

The Good Teacher's Almanac

please provide the following information:

Name: _____

Address: _____

City: _____ State: _____ Zip: _____

Telephone: _____

e-mail address: _____

Number of Copies Requested: _____

Fax orders: (973) 691-8477. Complete and send form.

e-mail orders: VAHPub@aol.com

Mail orders: Van Arsdale House Publishing
                126 Main Street
                Stanhope, NJ 07874

Shipping:
US: $4 for the first book, $2 for each additional book
Sales Tax will be added to all products shipped to NJ addresses.

Payment enclosed ☐   Please bill me ☐
Make checks payable to Van Arsdale House Publishing.

Please send FREE information on:
☐ Speaking   ☐ Seminars   ☐ Workshops

If you would like to order additional copies of

The Good Teacher's Almanac

please provide the following information:

Name: _____

Address: _____

City: _____ State: _____ Zip: _____

Telephone: _____

e-mail address: _____

Number of Copies Requested: _____

Fax orders: (973) 691-8477. Complete and send form.

e-mail orders: VAHPub@aol.com

Mail orders: Van Arsdale House Publishing
                126 Main Street
                Stanhope, NJ 07874

Shipping:
US: $4 for the first book, $2 for each additional book
Sales Tax will be added to all products shipped to NJ addresses.

Payment enclosed ☐   Please bill me ☐
Make checks payable to Van Arsdale House Publishing.

Please send FREE information on:
☐ Speaking   ☐ Seminars   ☐ Workshops

If you would like to order additional copies of

The Good Teacher's Almanac

please provide the following information:

Name: _____

Address: _____

City: _____ State: _____ Zip: _____

Telephone: _____

e-mail address: _____

Number of Copies Requested: _____

Fax orders: (973) 691-8477. Complete and send form.

e-mail orders: VAHPub@aol.com

Mail orders: Van Arsdale House Publishing
                126 Main Street
                Stanhope, NJ 07874

Shipping:
US: $4 for the first book, $2 for each additional book
Sales Tax will be added to all products shipped to NJ addresses.

Payment enclosed ☐   Please bill me ☐
Make checks payable to Van Arsdale House Publishing.

Please send FREE information on:
☐ Speaking ☐ Seminars ☐ Workshops

If you would like to order additional copies of

The Good Teacher's Almanac

please provide the following information:

Name: _____

Address: _____

City: _____ State: _____ Zip: _____

Telephone: _____

e-mail address: _____

Number of Copies Requested: _____

Fax orders: (973) 691-8477. Complete and send form.

e-mail orders: VAHPub@aol.com

Mail orders: Van Arsdale House Publishing
                126 Main Street
                Stanhope, NJ 07874

Shipping:
US: $4 for the first book, $2 for each additional book
Sales Tax will be added to all products shipped to NJ addresses.

Payment enclosed ☐   Please bill me ☐
Make checks payable to Van Arsdale House Publishing.

Please send FREE information on:
☐ Speaking   ☐ Seminars   ☐ Workshops